GOD'S HEART

WAYNE KOOPS

GOD'S HEART

Published by 21st Century Press
Springfield, MO 65807

21st Century Press is an evangelical Christian publisher dedicated to serving the local church with purpose books. We believe God's vision for 21st Century Press is to provide church leaders with biblical, user-friendly materials that will help them evangelize, disciple and minister to children, youth and families.

It is our prayer that this book will help you discover biblical truth for your own life and help you meet the needs of others. May God richly bless you.

21st Century Press
2131 W. Republic Rd.
PMB 211
Springfield, MO 65807
Email: Lee@21stcenturypress.com

Cover Design: Lee Fredrickson
Book Design: Lee Fredrickson

ISBN: 978-0-9863864-0-4
Visit our website at: www.21stcenturypress.com
Printed in the United States of America

21stCENTURY
P   R   E   S   S
READING YOU LOUD AND CLEAR

ACKNOWLEDGEMENTS

First I would like to thank my Heavenly Father, the amount of belief that you have in me after all the times that I have fallen in my life. You still believed in me and you still do, it is because I love your word so much and respect it for being the ultimate truth. I am so grateful and honored that you would think of me so highly enough to send your only son to die for me and for my sins so that I may have a relationship with you. Heavenly Father, I am nothing without you in my life. It is my deepest desire that even though I have failed you in so many ways and so many times. Each day I desire to get stronger and stronger because of you. At the end of it all I want to show you in any way that I can that I love you and that others may know you through me. In the end on that glorious day when we meet face to face; my ears might ring with joy at the sound of your glorious voice saying "Job well done my good and faithful servant!"

My second thanks and appreciation goes out to my dearest mother. Words cannot express how much you have shown me in this life in so many ways. Through the good and the bad, I have learned some of the most valuable lessons that couldn't have been taught more perfectly by anyone else but you. Your heart and your devotion towards the Lord is something that will continue to burn throughout the core of my being as long as I shall draw breathe on this earth. Know that the love that I have for you will always be in a very special spot in my heart. I will never forget you and everything that you have done and have shown me. I now know the value of never giving up and never surrendering no matter how hard it gets. Your courage and passion that you have implanted in me will continue to dwell with me for the rest of my days.

CONTENTS

INTRODUCTION

From all that I have become or could ever possibly be, I could have never imagined my life turning out the way that it did. I guess they say that there has to be a cost to create something, what was created in this book seems like it cost me my whole entire life, my family, my whole view on life and all the familiarities that were supposed to go along with it. To be perfectly clear this was never something that I wanted to write or create so to speak.

This book was started during a long dark series of events in my life. I wasn't even the original author; I was the spectator through it all. I was the one who watched this whole thing begin to unfold before my very eyes. I was there, when all the time and devotion and the research were put into this masterpiece. Little did I know that, at the time, I was being prepped as a student. At that point in my life; my relationship with the Lord was nowhere near what it needed to be at. I didn't have the kind of knowledge and wisdom it took to orchestrate God's word in such a profound way.

Little did I know that through that whole time of chaos and darkness in my life I was being prepared and trained for what God was planning for my life. When I look back at that time of my life, I will always say that it was out of the darkness that I was born and became. I truly believe with all my heart that the only way that I could truly understand God and understand his heart was to go through those trials in life. It wasn't until almost a decade after all those events, when the light had started to pierce through the darkness and in the stillness of all that was uncertain to me, my purpose and my future became clearer. I began to realize that it was this book, the context of it, that had opened up my eyes to see what life really was all about. I then, for the first time, had a real understanding of how all things had fit into place.

It wasn't until after my life had taken a totally different path, that the Lord started to convict me to finish something that was started so long ago. So with His help, and by being obedient to His voice, and being obedient to put down His words, I had finished this book and turned it into the finished product that He wanted. Once again the only thing I can take credit for in this book is having the obedience to create this book in the order that the Lord had wanted. The only reason why I wanted to have this book put out there for the world to see is because it is so amazing how after two thousand years of having a book like the Bible done in a certain way that the Lord can show you something totally different.

Something that I believe can change the path of mankind and his destiny. Through this book I believe that man can truly have a deep understanding of God and what his heart really is. I respect and cherish God's Word so much I couldn't give up on the idea that this could never get published. The passion for God's Word in this order is what has consumed me and continues to do so this day. I hope that you as a reader get all that you can out of this book. It truly was made for you. So that you could grow and you could learn and become stronger in your walk with God. So you could become more confident in who God is and how He works and how this crazy world works. Also, so that you could learn what is expected from you by God. My deepest desire is that through this book you will truly fall in love with Him and become the holy servant that you were meant to be.

Things to note as you read this book

All the scriptures used in this book came from the NIV version, there were a couple of verses that were taken from the King James Version. When you read this book I want you to realize that these scriptures were taken from all over the Bible and put in a particular order so that the subject that you are reading will be opened up to you in a way that has never been done before. All of this has been done for you. The Lord wants you to have a better understanding of Him and who He is.

Chapter One

Salvation

There are many different meanings to the word salvation. As people and human beings, can we really grasp the concept of having salvation? Without knowing and understanding what eternal separation from God feels like, how could anyone ever truly appreciate being rescued from something that they have never experienced? I want you to look back at your life and try to think of what was the most devastating thing that you have ever gone through. For a brief moment I want you to think of that situation. Do you remember the sadness that you felt, the agony, the pain, and the loss. Now I want you to take all of that, multiply it by a million, and you still haven't even scratched the surface of what you have been rescued from.

So I ask you this again, as a Christian, how can we have perspective on what it really means to have salvation? How is it possible that we can understand this? How do we really take hold and grasp this gift? There really is only one way that we can understand what salvation is and how it works. To get the whole picture we need to start at the beginning of time. Now we know that in the Bible it says in the beginning God created the earth and that He made man. We also know that He created us in His image (Genesis 1:26). So to get the right perspective let's take a look at this from a different view. Let's put you in God's seat to really see what is happening.

Now I want you to imagine yourself being God. It has been five days and you have been creating all kinds of magnificent things from the depths of what is within your spirit. You have made the heavens and the earth, the light and the darkness, the moon and the stars, the birds of the air and the fish of the sea, and all the creatures that roam the earth. It's the sixth day of you creating things and you have decided to save the best for last. Everything that you have created thus far is going to be minuscule compared to what is about to happen next.

You take a whole bunch of soil from the ground that you've just created and you start shaping and molding. Take a little off from here, add a little more for here and a little bit there, and fix this like so and there you have it. "It is perfect," you say to yourself, but wait, there is still something missing. Something needs to make this molding of clay come alive. Of course you need your breath of life, that very breathe that is from within your spirit. So you take a deep breath and close your eyes. You take from all that is inside your spirit as you breathe life on to your creation.

Then, at that very moment, you watch your creation open his eyes for the first time, and as he is opening his eyes he takes his very first breath of air, he even coughs a little as he is getting his lungs used to breathing for the very first time. While he stands there examining himself, trying to figure out what he is and how this happened, you gaze at him with joy.

There he is, standing before you, your beautiful creation of what was once a piece of clay from the ground and is now breathing and moving all on his own, all because of you. So here is this being, your creation, something that you had made, and you can't help but be so proud and love this man. You desire so much now to be a part of his life, you want to be able to share all that you are with this human being that you made. Just like being a parent, from that very first moment that you breathed life into your creation, you have felt love towards him. Why? He came from you.

Now as the creator you pour yourself into your loved one. You teach him all kinds of things; you give him all kinds of knowledge and understanding. You give him responsibilities and guidelines to keep him safe and protected because you don't want him to get hurt or have anything bad happen to him.

Most importantly you show him your love and the adoration you have towards him. As you begin to spend time with your man creation, you excitedly watch him learn and develop as he discovers things for the very first time. Now, however, there is one concern that you have and that is as time goes by you notice that something is wrong. You have given him this earth and everything in it, but as you interact with him daily you see that he feels alone and alienated from the rest of the species that you have created, so you suggest he find a mate and helper to be his companion along the way. Now, you know that as he searches for a companion that he isn't going to find a suitable helper for himself; but you let him search anyway and as he searches he finds that all the other animals have one of their own kind made just for them, and yet he doesn't.

So you take your man that you created and put him into a deep sleep. You take the flesh and bone from his body and you create something anew and beautiful. She is exquisite like your creation, she is human as well, yet she is made different. She is made just to suit his needs. You did this in such a way so that the two can become one, created as if they were meant to be together. So your man is sleeping, and when he awakes you show him his life-long partner. Now your beloved creation is complete. He has everything he needs, a purpose, companionship and time that he gets to share with you. Finally everything is set for the rest of eternity.

So now your whole world that you have created brings glory to you and you're enjoying all the things that you have made. Everything that is in existence is perfect. All is well until one day, when you go to meet up with the man and woman, you can't find them. They are not where they usually are. This is a little strange and unusual, so you go to search for them. As you are searching you call out to them. Finally you locate them and you notice that they look different and they are acting kind of strange. As this is happening your heart begins to break as you understand that the reason they are acting different is because they broke one of the rules that you had given them to live by. What saddens you even more is that because they broke that rule they have now guaranteed themselves separation from you. Now you can't interact with them like you use to and one day they will be completely out of your life for good. You see, they now have sin in their life and it will kill them and destroy them.

Imagine seeing your child, whom you've raised, be given the death sentence. You know now that one day you won't be able to see them anymore. They will be gone out of your life forever. Only to be a distant memory of the time you have invested in them. No matter what your child has done you will always love them. You would do anything for them, because you love them. You cherish them, they are your world.

Now you know what it is like to be God. God had to come up with a game plan, a strategy, something. He couldn't let His creation die like this; NO! NO! He loved them too much! So what did He do? He did what any loving parent would do for their child. He stood in their place! So in order to really understand what salvation is: you have to look at it from a parent's perspective. The true definition of salvation is to salvage what was once lost in love. That is what God's purpose has been since the beginning of time.

Wisdom from God's Heart

"When you have lifted up the son of man, then you will know that I am he and that I do nothing on my own but speak just what the father has taught me." -John 8:28 "The one who sent me is with me: he has not left me alone, for I always do what pleases him." -John 8:29 "The reason my father loves me is that I lay down my life only to take it up again. No one takes it from me, but I lay it down of my own accord. I have authority to lay it down and authority to take it up again. This command I have received from my father." -John 10:17-18

"The world must learn that I love the father and I do exactly what the father has commanded me." -John 14:31 "By myself I can do nothing; I judge only as I hear, for I seek not to please myself but him who sent me." -John 5:30 During the days of Jesus' life on earth, he offered up prayers and petitions with loud cries and tears to the one who could save him from death, and he was heard because of his reverent submission. Although he was a son, he learned obedience from what he suffered and, once made perfect, he became the source of eternal salvation for all who obey him. -Hebrews 5:7-9 Jesus Christ died for all, that those who live should no longer live for themselves but for him who died for them and was raised again. -2 Corinthians 5.15

For God so loved the world that he gave his one and only son, that whoever believes in him shall not perish but have eternal life. For God did not send his son to condemn the world, but to save the world through him. Whoever believes in him is not condemned, but whoever does not believe stands condemned already because he has not believed in the name of God's one and only son. This is the verdict: light has come into the world, but men loved darkness instead of light because their deeds were evil. Everyone who does evil hates light, and will not come into the light for fear that his deeds will be exposed. But whoever lives by the truth comes into the light, so that it may be seen plainly that what he has done has been done through God. -John 3:16-21

Who has believed our message and to whom has the arm of the Lord been revealed? He grew up before him like a tender shoot, and like a root out of dry ground. He had no beauty or majesty to attract us to him, nothing in his appearance that we should desire him. He was despised and rejected by men, a man of sorrows, and familiar with pain. Like one from who men hide their faces he was despised and we esteemed him not. Surely he took up our infirmities and carried our sorrows, yet we considered him stricken by God, smitten by him, and afflicted. But he was pierced for our transgressions, he was crushed for our iniquities; the punishment that brought us peace was on him, and by his wounds we are healed. We all, like sheep, have gone astray, each of us has turned to his own way; and the Lord had laid on him the iniquity of us all. He was oppressed and afflicted, yet he did not open his mouth; he was led like a lamb to the slaughter, as a sheep before her shearers is silent, so he did not open his mouth. By oppression and judgment he was taken away. And who can speak of his descendants? For he was cut off the land of the living; for the transgressions of my people he was stricken. He was assigned a grave with the wicked and with the rich in his death, though he had done no violence, nor was any deceit in his mouth. Yet it was the Lord's will to crush him and cause him to suffer, and though the Lord makes his life a guilt offering, he will see his offspring and prolong his days, and the will of the Lord will prosper in his hand. After the suffering of his soul, he will see the light of life and be satisfied; by his knowledge my righteous servant will justify many, and he will bear their iniquities. Therefore I will give him a portion among the great, and he will divide the spoils with the strong, because he poured out his life unto death, and was numbered with transgressors. For he bore the sin of many, and made intercession for the transgressors. -Isaiah 53 God demonstrates his own love for us in this: while we were still sinners, Christ died for us. Since we have now been justified by his blood, how much more shall we be saved from God's wrath through him. -Romans 5:8-9 For he has rescued us from the dominion of darkness and brought us into the kingdom of the son he loves. -Colossians 1:13 God made him who had no sin to be sin for us, so that in him we might become the righteousness of God. -2 Corinthians 5:21

Now Christ has appeared once for all at the end of the ages to do away with sin by the sacrifice of himself. Just as man is destined to die once, and after that to face judgment, so Christ was sacrificed once to take away the sins of many people; and he will appear a second time, not to bear sin, but to bring salvation to those who are waiting for him. -Hebrews 9:26-28 In Christ we have redemption through his blood, the forgiveness of sins, in accordance with the riches of God's grace that he lavished on us. With all wisdom and understanding, he made known to us the mystery of his will according to his good pleasure, which he purposed in Christ, to be put in to effect when the times will have reached their fulfillment to bring all things in heaven and on earth together under one head, even Christ. -Ephesians 1:7-10

Once you were alienated from God and were enemies in your minds because of your evil behavior. But now he has reconciled you by Christ's physical body through death to present you holy in his sight, without blemish and free from accusation, if you continue in your faith, established and firm, not moved from the hope held out in the gospel. -Colossians 1:21-23 When you were dead in your sins and in the uncircumcision of your sinful nature, God made you alive with Christ. He forgave us all our sins, having cancelled the written code, with its regulations, that was against us and that stood opposed to us; he took it away, nailing it to the cross. And having disarmed the powers and authorities, he made a public spectacle of them, triumphing over them by the cross. -Colossians 2:13-15 Therefore, if anyone is in Christ, he is a new creation: the old is gone, the new has come! All this from God, who reconciled us to himself through Christ and gave us the ministry of reconciliation: that God was reconciling the world to himself in Christ, not counting men's sins against them. -2 Corinthians 5:17-19

For God was pleased to have all fullness dwell in Christ, and through Christ to reconcile himself all things, whether things on earth or things in heaven, by making peace through his blood. -Colossians 1:19-20 Through Christ (both Jews and gentiles) have access to the father by one spirit. Consequently, you are no longer foreigners and aliens, but fellow citizens with God's people and members of God's household, built on the foundation of the apostles and prophets, with Christ Jesus himself as the chief cornerstone. In him the whole building is joined together and rises to become a holy temple in the Lord. And in him you too are being built together to become a dwelling in which God lives by his spirit. - Ephesians 2:18-22 Here is a trustworthy saying that deserves full acceptance: Christ Jesus came into the world to save sinners of who I am the worst. But for that very reason I was shown mercy so that in me, the worst of sinners, Christ Jesus might display his unlimited patience as an example for those who would believe on him and receive eternal life. -1 Timothy 1:15-16

So do not be ashamed to testify about our Lord or ashamed of me his prisoner. But join with me in suffering for the gospel, by the power of God. Who has saved us and called us to a holy life, not because of anything we have done but because of his own purpose and grace. This grace was given us in Christ Jesus before the beginning of time, but it has now been revealed through the appearing of our savior,

Christ Jesus, who has destroyed death and has brought life and immortality to light through the gospel. -2 Timothy 1:8-10

For the grace of God that brings salvation has appeared to all men. -Titus 2:11 If you confess with your mouth, "Jesus is Lord," and believe in your heart that God raised him from the dead, you will be saved. For it is with your heart that you believe and are justified, and it is with your mouth that you confess and are saved. As the scripture says, "anyone who trusts in him will never be put to shame." For there is no difference between Jew and gentile, the same Lord is Lord of all and richly blesses all who call on him, for "everyone who calls on the name of the Lord will be saved." -Romans 10:9-13 "Come to me, all you who are weary and burdened, and I will give you rest. Take my yoke upon you and learn from me, for I am gentle and humble in heart, and you will find rest for your souls. For my yoke is easy and my burden is light. -Matthew 11:28-30

"If anyone would come after me, he must deny himself and take up his cross and follow me. For whoever wants to save his life will lose it, but whoever loses his life for me will find it. What good will it be for a man if he gains the whole world, yet forfeits his soul? Or what can a man give in exchange for his soul? For the son of man is going to come in his father's glory with his angels, and then he will reward each person according to what he has done." -Matthew 16:24-27 "Whoever acknowledges me before men, I will also acknowledge him before my father in heaven. But whoever disowns me before men, I will disown him before my father in heaven." -Matthew 10:32-33

"I tell you the truth, unless you eat the flesh of the son of man and drink his blood, you have no life in you. Whoever eats my flesh and drinks my blood has eternal life, and I will raise him up at the last day. For my flesh is real food and my blood is real drink. Whoever eats my flesh and drinks my blood remains in me, and I in him. Just as the living father sent me and I live because of the father, so the one who feeds on me will live because of me. This is the bread that came down from heaven. Your forefathers ate manna and died, but he who feeds on this bread will live forever." - John 6:53-58

"Whoever has my commands and obeys them, he is the one who loves me. The one who loves me will be loved by my father. I too will love him and show myself to him. If anyone loves me he will obey my teaching. My father will love him, and we will come to him and make our home with him." -John 14:21, 23 "As the father has loved me, so I have loved you. Now remain in my love! If you obey my commands, you will remain in my love, just as I have obeyed my father's commands and remain in his love. I have told you this so that my joy may be in you and that your joy may be complete." -John 15:9-11

"I am the vine; and you are the branches. If a man remains in me and I in him, he will bear much fruit; apart from me you can do nothing. If anyone does not remain in me, he is like a branch that is thrown away and withers; such branches are picked up, thrown into the fire and burned." -John 15:5-6 "I tell you the truth, no one can see the kingdom of God unless he is born again. Unless he is born of water and spirit. Flesh gives birth to flesh, but the spirit gives birth to spirit." -John 3:3, 5-6 "The spirit gives life; the flesh counts for nothing. The words I have spoken to you are spirit and they are life." -John 6:63 "I tell you the truth, if anyone keeps my word he will never see death." -John 8:51 "If anyone is thirsty, let him come to me and drink. Whoever believes in me, as the scripture has said, streams of living water will flow from within him." -John 7:37-38 Repent and be baptized, every one of you, in the name of Jesus Christ for the forgiveness of your sins. And you will receive the gift of the Holy Spirit. -Acts 2:38 "The counselor, the Holy Spirit, whom the father will send in my name, will teach you all things and will remind you of everything I have taught you." -John 14:26 "Hear I am! I stand at the door and knock. If anyone hears my voice and opens the door, I will come in and eat with him, and he with me. To him who overcomes, I will give the right to sit with me on my throne, just as I overcame and sat down with the father on his throne." -Revelation 3:20-21

Questions for Reflection and Discussion

1. In your own words, what does it mean for YOU to live out your salvation?

2. What are some ideas of ways that YOU could live out your life so that others might recognize that you are saved?

3. Think for a moment and identify what are the areas or things in your life that YOU might need to deny or prioritize and lay down before the Lord?

4. Are there things that you put on a higher scale than God? If so, list them.

5. At this point in your life, are you 100% sure that you have salvation, and that if you died this moment your name would be written in the book of life? If not, what do you think needs to be done or fixed so that you will have that assurance?

CHAPTER TWO

SIN

Sin is devastating. Sin is what made that young man rob a bank. Sin is what made that young girl lie to her parents so she could be out having sex with her boyfriend. Sin made that young college boy rape that girl at the party when he was drunk. Sin made that man kill another man because he looked at him the wrong way. Sin made that woman shoplift that designer dress she is wearing. Sin is everywhere. It is the most disastrous three-letter word in the whole English language. Being a Christian, you understand the topic of sin is a huge part of your life. Sin is the thing you struggle with the most. Why do people have to struggle with sin so much? Why is it so hard to do good? Why is it so appealing and fun to sin? Why does there always have to be so many temptations that we have to face? These may be some of the questions that you have asked yourself at one point in your life.

To understand sin and how it works there are a few key principles that you are going to have to understand in order to see the big picture behind sin and how it operates. The first thing you need to realize and understand is: as long as you live in this world you will never be able to escape sin. Sin is, and always will be, around you for the rest of your life. Sin is a part of you, it is embedded in your nature, and you were born into the nature of sin.

However, once you accept the fact that there is no escaping sin and that you never were, nor will you ever be, perfect and sinless, then you have taken steps in the right direction. What you have to realize is that just because you can't escape the sin or the sinful nature that you were born into, does not mean that you are a slave to sin and that you have to obey its every desire that it may have for you. Once you realize that you have sin in your life and sin will always be a temptation, you can turn and look towards redemption; which is in Jesus Christ. Because of what Jesus Christ did on the cross, sin does not have reign over you anymore. Also, because Jesus paid the price for your sins this gives you the ability to overcome your sinful nature once and for all.

With that being said, because sin is in the world; every man, woman and child will have to pay a price, and that price is death. We will all die at some point in time, but the good news is that because of Jesus paying the atonement for our sins, we no longer have to fear eternal separation from God the Father. In fact because of what Jesus did we not only have the freedom to refuse to sin, but we have the ability to keep our relationship established with God the Father as we go through our lives.

This gives us the freedom to live for Him and not for sin. Knowing that you are forgiven of your sins is a great confidence we should all have as Christians. When it comes to sin, our biggest responsibility is this: that we choose daily to live for Christ and not for our own evil desires.

Wisdom from God's Heart

For all have sinned and fall short of the glory of God, and are justified freely by his grace through the redemption that came by Christ Jesus. -Romans 3:23-25 Who can say "I have kept my heart pure; I am clean without sin?" -Proverbs 20:9 As it is written: "There is none righteous, not even one; there is no one who understands; no one who seeks God. All have turned away, they have together become worthless; there is no one who does good, not even one." -Romans 3:10-12 Surely I was sinful at birth, sinful from the time my mother conceived me. -Psalm 51:5

Therefore, just as sin entered the world through one man, and death through sin, and in this way death came to all men, because all have sinned. -Romans 5:12 But the scripture declares that the whole world is a prisoner of sin, so that what was promised, being given through faith in Jesus Christ, might be given to those who believe. -Galatians 3:22 The acts of sinful nature are obvious: sexual immorality, impurity and debauchery; idolatry and witchcraft; hatred, discord, jealousy, fits of rage, selfish ambition, dissensions, factions and envy, drunkenness, orgies and the like. I warn you as I did before, that those who live like this will not enter the kingdom of heaven. -Galatians 5:19-21 Flee from sexual immorality. All other sins a man commits outside his body, but he who sins sexually, sins against his own body. -1 Corinthians 6:18

The love of money is the root of all evil. Some people, eager for money, have wandered from the faith and pierced themselves with many griefs! -1 Timothy 6:10 You want something but you don't get it. You kill and covet, but you cannot have what you want. You quarrel and fight. You do not have because you do not ask God. When you ask, you do not receive, because you ask with wrong motives, that you may spend what you get on your pleasures. You adulterous people, don't you know that friendship with the world is hatred towards God? Anyone who chooses to be a friend to the world becomes an enemy of God. - James 4:2-4

If anyone teaches false doctrines and does not agree to the sound instruction of our Lord Jesus Christ and to godly teaching, he is conceited and understands nothing. He has an unhealthy interest in controversies and quarrels about words that result in envy, strife, malicious talk, evil suspicions and constant friction between men of corrupt mind, who have been robbed of the truth and who think that godliness is a means to financial gain. -1 Timothy 6:3-5 Do not be misled; bad company corrupts good character. -1 Corinthians 15:33 Haughty eyes and a proud heart, the lamp of the wicked are sin. -Proverbs 21:4 When words are many, sin is not absent, but he who holds his tongue is wise. -Proverbs 10:19

In your anger do not sin. Do not let the sun go down while you are still angry, and do not give the devil a foothold. -Ephesians 4:26-27 In your anger do not sin, when you are on your beds, search your hearts and be silent. -Psalm 4:4 If you really keep the royal law found in scripture, "love your neighbor as yourself," you are doing right. But if you show favoritism, you sin and are convicted by the law as lawbreakers. -James 2:8-9

Anyone who does not love remains in death. Anyone who hates his brother is a murderer, and you know that no murderer has eternal life in him. – 1 John 3:14-15

Anyone, then, who knows the good he ought to do and doesn't do it, sins. -James 4:17 Fools mock at making amends for sin, but goodwill is found among the upright. -Proverbs 14:9 Do not be deceived: God cannot be mocked. A man reaps what he sows. The one who sows to please his sinful nature, from that nature will reap destruction; the one who sows to please the spirit, from the spirit will reap eternal life. -Galatians 6:7-8

He who does what is sinful is of the devil, because the devil has been sinning from the beginning. The reason the Son of God appeared was to destroy the devil's work. -1 John 3:8 This is the message we have heard from him and declare to you: God is light; in him there is no darkness at all. If we claim to have fellowship with him yet walk in the darkness, we lie and do not live by the truth. But if we walk in the light, as he is in the light, we have fellowship with one another, and the blood of Jesus, his son, purifies us from all sin. If we claim to be without sin, we deceive ourselves and the truth is not in us. If we confess our sins, he is faithful and just and will forgive us our sins and purify us from all unrighteousness. If we claim we have not sinned, we make him out to be a liar and his word has no place in our lives. -1 John 1: 5-10

For the wages of sin is death, but the gift of God is eternal life in Christ Jesus our lord! -Romans 6:23 "I tell you the truth, everyone who sins is a slave to sin. Now a slave has no permanent place in the family, but a son belongs to it forever. So if the son sets you free, you will be free indeed." -John 8:34-36 Consequently, just as the result of one trespass was condemnation for all men, so also the result of one act of righteousness was justification that brings life for all men. For just as through disobedience of the one man the many were made sinners, so also through the obedience of the one man many will be made righteous. -Romans 5:18-19 But the gift is not like the trespass. For if the many died by the trespass of one man, how much more did God's grace and the gift that came by the grace of one man, Jesus Christ, overflow to the many. -Romans 5:15

Therefore, there is now no condemnation for those who are in Christ Jesus, because through Christ Jesus the law of the spirit of life set me free from the law of sin and death. -Romans 8:1-2 But if Christ is in you, your body is dead because of sin, yet your spirit is alive because of righteousness. If the spirit of him who raised Jesus from the dead is living in you, He who raised Christ from the dead will also give you life to your mortal bodies through his spirit who lives in you. -Romans 8:10-11 God made him who had no sin to be sin for us, so that in him we might become the righteousness of God. -2 Corinthians 5:21 For we do not have a high priest who is unable to sympathize with our weaknesses, but we have one who has been tempted in every way, just as we are yet without sin. -Hebrews 4:15 So Christ was sacrificed once to take away the sins of many people; and he will appear a second time. Not to bear sin, but to bring salvation to those who are waiting for him. -Hebrews 9:28

To this you were called, because Christ suffered for you, leaving you an example, that you should follow in his steps. "He committed no sin, and no deceit was found in his mouth." -1 Peter 2:21-22 Therefore, Christ suffered in his body, arm yourselves also with the same attitude, because he who has suffered in his body is done with sin. As a result, he does not live the rest of his earthly body for evil human desires, but rather for the will of God. -1 Peter 4:1-2

My dear children, I write this to you so that you will not sin. But if anybody does sin, we have one who speaks to the father in our defense Jesus Christ, the righteous one. He is the atoning sacrifice for our sins, and not only for ours but also for the sins of the whole world. -1 John 2:1-2

"And so I tell you, every sin and blasphemy will be forgiven men, blasphemy against the spirit will not be forgiven. Anyone who speaks a word against the son of man will be forgiven, but anyone who speaks against the Holy Spirit will not be forgiven, either in this age or the age to come. -Matthew 12:31-32

"But I tell you the truth, it is for your good that I am going away. Unless I go away, the counselor will not come to you; when he comes, he will convict the world of guilt in regard to sin and righteousness and judgment: In regard to sin, because men do not believe in me." -John 16:7-9

If we deliberately keep on sinning after we have received the knowledge of the truth, no sacrifice for sins is left, but only a fearful expectation of judgment and raging fire that will consume the enemies of God. -Hebrews 10:26-27 What then? Shall we sin because we are not under the law but under grace? By no means! Don't you know that when you offer yourselves to someone to obey him as slaves, you are slaves to the one whom you obey, whether you are slaves to sin, which leads to death, or to obedience, which leads to righteousness? But thanks be to God that, though you used to be slaves to sin, you wholeheartedly obeyed the form of teaching to which you were entrusted. You have been set free from sin and have become slaves to righteousness. -Romans 6:15-18

Everyone who sins breaks the law; in fact, sin is lawlessness. But you know that he appeared so that he might take away our sins. And in him is no sin. No one who lives in him keeps on sinning. No one who continues to sin has either seen him or known him. -1 John 3:4-6 When tempted, no one should say "God is tempting me." For God cannot be tempted by evil, nor does he tempt anyone; but each one is tempted when by his own evil desires, he is dragged away and enticed. -James 1:13-14 For if you live according to the sinful nature, you will die; but if by the spirit you put to death the misdeeds of the body, you will live. Those who are led by the spirit of God are sons of God. -Romans 8:13-14

Do you know that your body is a temple of the Holy Spirit, who is in you, whom you have received from God? You are not your own; You were bought at a price. Therefore honor God with your body. -1 Corinthians 6:19-20 It is impossible for those who have been once enlightened, and who have tasted the heavenly gift, who have shared in the Holy Spirit, who have tasted the goodness of the word of God and the powers of the coming age. If they fall away to be brought back to repentance, because to their loss they are crucifying the Son of God all over again and subjecting him to public disgrace.-Hebrews 6:4-6

The man who says "I know him," but does not do what he commands is a liar, and the truth is not in him. If anyone obeys his word, God's love is truly made complete in him. This is how we know we are in him: whoever claims to live in him must walk as Jesus did. -1 John 2:4-6 If a righteous man turns from his righteousness and commits sin and does the same detestable thing the wicked man does, will he live? None of the righteous things he has done will be remembered. Because of the unfaithfulness he is guilty of and because of the sins he has committed, he will die! - Ezekiel 18:24

No one who is born of God will continue to sin, because God's seed remains in him; he cannot go on sinning, because he has been born of God. This is how we know who the children of the devil are: anyone who does not do what is right is not a child of God, nor is anyone who does not love his brother. -1 John 3:9-10

God's solid foundation stands firm, sealed with this inscription: "The Lord knows those who are his," and, "Everyone who confesses the name of the Lord must turn away from wickedness!" -2 Timothy 2:19 Repent, then, and turn to God, so that your sins may be wiped out, that times of refreshing may come from the Lord. Be baptized every one of you, in the name of Jesus Christ for the forgiveness of your sins. -Acts 3:19, 2:38 Those of us who are baptized into Christ Jesus are also baptized into his death. -Romans 6:3

For we know that our old self was crucified with him so that the body of sin might be done away with, that we should no longer be slaves to sin, because anyone who had died has been freed from sin. Now if we died with Christ, we believe that we shall also live with him. For we know that since Christ was raised from the dead, he cannot die again; death no longer has mastery over him. The death he died, he died to sin once for all; but the life he lives, he lives to God. In the same way, count yourself dead to sin but alive to God in Christ Jesus. Therefore do not let sin reign in your mortal body so that you obey its evil desires. Do not offer the parts of your body to sin as instruments of wickedness, but rather offer yourselves to God as those who have been brought from death to life; and offer the parts of your body to him as instruments of righteousness. - Romans 6:6-13

The fruit of the spirit is love, joy, peace, patience, kindness, goodness, faithfulness, gentleness and self-control. Against such there is no law. Those who belong to Christ Jesus have crucified the sinful nature with its passions and desires. -Galatians 5:22-24 For God has not given us a spirit of fear: but of power, and of love, and of a sound mind. -2 Timothy 1:7 For this reason I remind you to fan into flame the gift of God, which is in you through the laying on of my hands. -2 Timothy 1:6 For you did not receive a spirit that makes you a slave again to fear, but you received the spirit of sonship. And by him we cry, "Abba Father." -Romans 8:15

The sins of some men are obvious, reaching the place of judgment ahead of them; The sins of others trail behind them. In the same way, good deeds are obvious, and even those that are not cannot be hidden. -1 Timothy 5:24-25 Peter came to Jesus and asked "Lord, how many times should I forgive my brother when he sins against me? Up to seven times?" Jesus answered, "I tell you, not seven times but seventy-seven times." -Matthew 18:21-22 But encourage one another daily, as long as it is called "today," so that none of you may be hardened by sins deceitfulness. -Hebrews 3:13

To the pure, all things pure, but to those who are corrupted and do not believe, nothing is pure. In fact, both their minds and consciences are corrupted. They claim to know God, but their actions deny him. -Titus 1:15-16 "You are the salt of the earth. But if the salt loses its saltiness, how can it be made salty again? It is no longer good for anything, except to be thrown out and trampled by men." -Matthew 5:13

Blessed is he whose transgressions are forgiven, whose sins are covered. Blessed is the man whose sin the Lord does not count against him and in whose spirit is no deceit. -Psalm 32:1-2 I have hidden your word in my heart that I might not sin against you. Praise be to you, oh Lord, teach me your decrees. -Psalm 119:11-12 I said, "I will watch my ways and keep my tongue from sin." -Psalm 39:1

Then I acknowledged my sin to you and did not cover up my iniquity. I said, "I will confess my transgressions to the Lord and you forgave me the guilt of my sin." -Psalm 32:5 Righteousness exalts a nation, but sin is a disgrace to any people. -Proverbs 14:34

Questions for Reflection and Discussion

1. List four different ways that can help you to keep sin out of your life.

2. Do you have an accountability partner that you share the sins that you struggle with? If not, do you think an accountability person would be beneficial to you?

3. List the sins that you struggle with in your life.

4. Find two scriptures for each type of sin that you are dealing with. Explain how these scriptures can help you get over your sin.

5. How much time do you spend in the Bible and in prayer? Do you think the time you spend is enough to help you overcome the sins that you are dealing with?

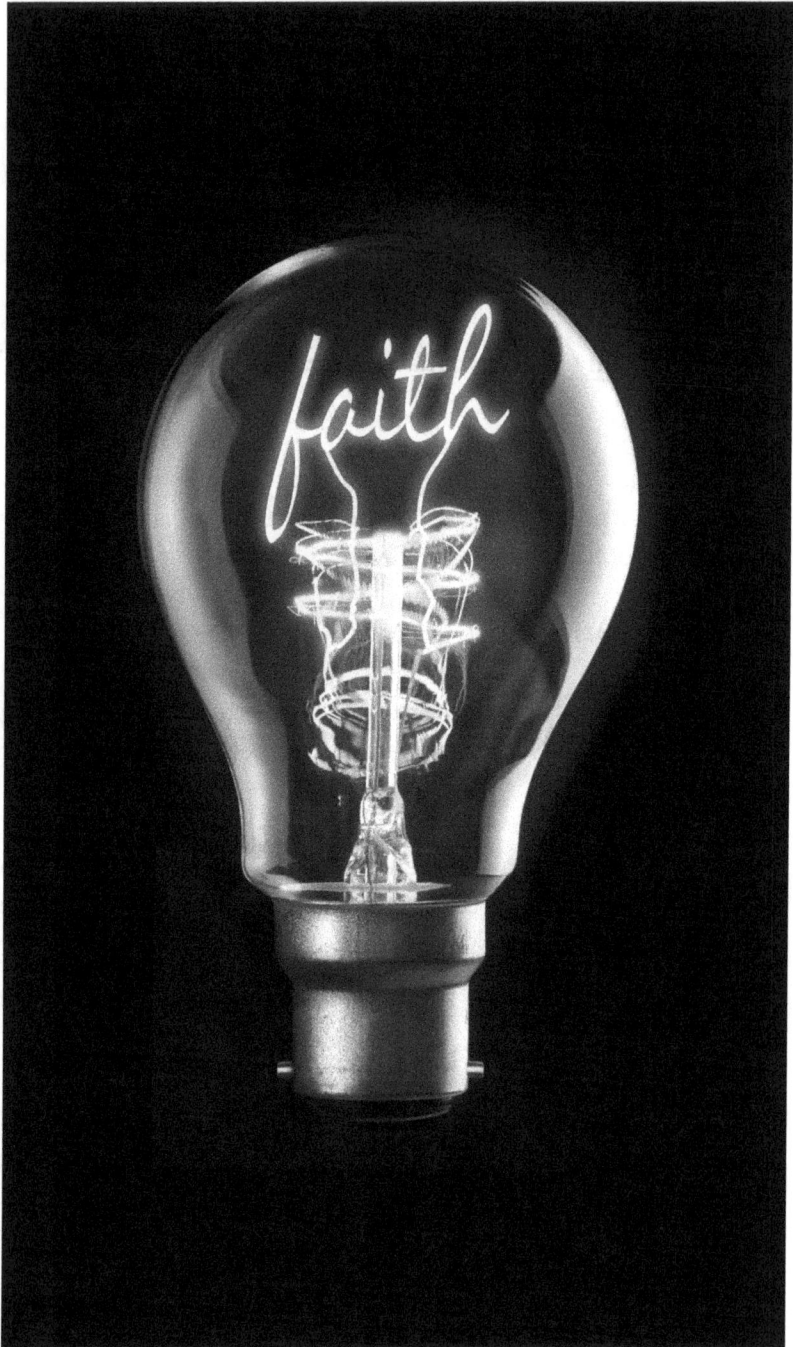

CHAPTER THREE

FAITH

What can we say about faith with a world like the one we live in today? In today's society, we have access to anything we want; anything we desire. We are living in a fix it generation where it literally is every man, woman and child for themselves. We live in a microwave generation, where we want to have everything instantly, and in most cases that is how it happens. The sad thing is, if you ask most people what faith is they will tell you it is what you believe in and that's it. So many people in this world are searching for something, whether it is carnal pleasures or a deeper meaning to life. In today's society people have become complacent with many different beliefs or faiths. So what is Faith? What does faith mean as a Christian in today's Society?

First of all the biggest misconception of faith is that it has to do with just something you believe in. Children believe in Santa Clause, the tooth fairy and the Easter bunny, but does that make them real? No, not at all! We all know that those things don't exist. So there has to be more to faith then just belief, but what is it? What does it mean to have faith in God? How do you acquire faith in God, Jesus and the Holy Spirit? The first thing you have to understand about faith is although it does have partly to do with believing in something, faith is not something you can just have instantly. No, faith is a foundation that you build and great faith isn't something you can achieve overnight. Faith is a foundation that you build over a lifetime. From the moment you make that decision to commit your life to Christ, until the day you take your last breath here on this earth, faith is working in your life.

The next thing you have to realize about faith is, faith does not exist unless there are actions to back it up. That is where building your foundation comes into place. If you claim to have faith in God, Jesus, and the Holy Spirit, then your actions, the things you say and do, have to back up what you believe. That's why it makes no sense when people say, "I'm a Christian," but then you ask them when was the last time they read the Bible and they say, "Oh, it's been a while and yeah I don't read it as often as I should." Well, if the Bible is the biggest tool that you have, then shouldn't you have that thing memorized if that is truly what you believe in?

We know the saying, "Actions speak louder than words." Which is true when it comes to faith in the Lord. In order to have faith in God, you have to have actions to back it up. The only way you can have actions to back it up is finding out what it is He wants you to do for Him. I mean that makes sense right? If you love God, then you want to find out what it is that pleases Him, right? That is why you spend time praying to Him and reading the Bible, His words for you. Just remember this: true faith requires action; that action will be a result of your love to God; those actions will make a difference in this world!

Wisdom from God's Heart

Examine yourselves to see whether you are in the faith; test yourselves. Do you not realize that Christ Jesus is in you? Unless, of course, you fail the test. -2 Corinthians 13:5 Anyone who does not provide for his relatives, especially for his immediate family, he had denied the faith and is worse than an unbeliever. -1 Timothy 5:8 Therefore, as we have opportunity, let us do good to all people, especially to those in the household of faith. - Galatians 6:9 KJV Neither do we go beyond our limits by boasting of work done by others. Our hope is that, as your faith continues to grow, our area of activity among you will greatly expand. -2 Corinthians 10:15 But just as you excel in everything; in faith, in speech, in knowledge, in complete earnestness and in your love for us, see that you also excel in this grace of giving. -2 Corinthians 8:7

Clearly no one is justified before God by the law, because "The righteous will live by faith." -Galatians 3:11   Once you were alienated from God and were enemies in your minds because of your evil behavior. But now he has reconciled you by Christ's physical body through death to present you holy in his sight, without blemish and free from accusation. If you continue in your faith, established and firm, not moved from the hope held out in the gospel. -Colossians 1:21-25   It is written: "I believed; therefore I have spoken." With that same spirit of faith, we also believe and therefore speak. -2 Corinthians 4:13

Be on your guard; stand firm in the faith; be men of courage; be strong. Do everything in love. -1 Corinthians 16:13-14   If I have the gift of prophecy and can fathom all mysteries and all knowledge, and if I have a faith that can move mountains, but not have love, I am nothing. -1 Corinthians 13:2   For we live by faith, not by sight. -2 Corinthians 5:7

Therefore, since we have been justified through faith, we have peace with God through our Lord Jesus Christ. Through whom we have gained access by faith into this grace which we now stand. And we rejoice in the hope of the glory of God. Not only so, but we also rejoice in our sufferings, because we know that suffering produces perseverance; perseverance, character; and character, hope. And hope does not disappoint us, because God has poured out his love into our hearts by the Holy Spirit, whom he has given us. -Romans 5:1-5

But you, dear friends, build yourselves up in your most holy faith and pray in the Holy Spirit. -Jude 1:20   For in the gospel a righteousness from God is revealed, a righteousness that is by faith from first to last, just as it is written: " The righteous will live by faith." -Romans 1:17   Consequently, faith comes from hearing the message, and the message is heard through the word of Christ. -Romans 10:17   Through him and for his name's sake, received grace and apostleship to call people from among all the gentiles to the obedience that comes from faith. -Romans 1:5   For this reason, ever since I heard about your faith in the Lord Jesus and your love for all the saints. I have not stopped giving thanks for you, remembering you in my prayers. -Ephesians 1:15-16

Though I am absent from you in body. I am present with you in spirit and delight to see how orderly you are and how firm your faith in Christ is. -Colossians 2:5   We continually remember before our God and father your worked produced by faith, labor prompted by love, and your endurance inspired by hope in our Lord Jesus Christ. -1 Thessalonians 1:3   The Lord's message rang out from you not only in Macedonia and Achia. Your faith in God has become known everywhere. - 1 Thessalonians 1:8

Therefore, brothers, in our distress and persecution we were encouraged about you because of you faith. -1 Thessalonians 3:7   We ought always to thank God for you brothers, and rightly so, because your faith is growing more and more, and the love every one of you have for each other is increasing. -2 Thessalonians 1:3   But by faith we eagerly await through the spirit the righteousness for which we hope. -Galatians 5:5   That is, that you and I may be mutually encouraged by each other's faith. -Romans 1:12

Remember your leaders, who spoke the word of God to you. Consider the outcome of their way of life and imitate their faith. -Hebrews 13:7   Let us fix our eyes on Jesus, the author and perfecter of our faith. Who for the joy set before him endured the cross, scorning its shame, and sat down at the right hand of the throne of God. -Hebrews 12:2 For, in just a very little while, "He who is coming will come and will not delay, but my righteous one will live by faith, and if he shrinks back, I will not be pleased with him." But we are not of those who shrink back and are destroyed, but of those who believe and are saved. -Hebrews 10:37-39

We do not want you to be lazy, but to imitate those who through faith and patience inherit what has been promised. -Hebrews 6:12   I pray that you may be active in sharing your faith so that you will have a full understanding of every good thing we have in Christ. -Philemon 1:6   As the body without the spirit is dead, so faith without deeds is dead. -James 2:26   What good is it, my brothers, if a man claims to have faith but has no deeds? Can such faith save?

Suppose a brother or sister is without clothes and daily food. If one of you says to him, "Go, I wish you well; keep warm and well fed," But does nothing about his physical needs, what good is it? In the same way, faith by itself, if it is not accompanied by action, is dead. -James 2:14-17 But someone will say, "You have faith; I have deeds." Show me your faith without deeds, and I will show you my faith by what I do. -James 2:18

You see that a person is justified by what he does and not by faith alone. -James 2:24 For we also have had the gospel preached to us, just as they did; but the message they heard was of no value to them, because those who heard did not combine it with faith. -Hebrews 4:2 Flee the evil desires of youth and pursue righteousness, faith, love and peace. Along with those who call on the Lord out of a pure heart. -2 Timothy 2:22 With this in mind, we constantly pray for you, that our God may count you worthy of his calling, and that by his power he may fulfill every good purpose of yours and every act prompted by your faith. -2 Thessalonians 1:11

Fight the good fight of faith. Take hold of the eternal life to which you were called when you made your good confession in the presence of many witnesses. -1 Timothy 6:12 I have fought the good fight, I have finished the race, I have kept the faith. -2 Timothy 4:7 My message and my preaching were not with wise and persuasive words, but with a demonstration of the Spirit's power, so that your faith might not rest on men's wisdom, but on God's power. -1 Corinthians 2:4-5 In this you greatly rejoice, though now for a little while you may have had to suffer grief in all kinds of trials. These have come so that your faith, of greater worth than gold, which perishes even though refined by fire. May be proved genuine and may result in praise, glory and honor when Jesus Christ is revealed. -1 Peter 1:6-7

Be self-controlled and alert, your enemy the devil prowls around like a roaring lion looking for someone to devour. Resist him, standing firm in the faith, because you know that your brothers throughout the world are undergoing the same kind of sufferings. -1 Peter 5:8-9 For this very reason, make every effort to add to your faith goodness; and to goodness, knowledge; and to knowledge, self-control; and to self-control, perseverance; and to perseverance, godliness; and to godliness, brotherly kindness; and to brotherly kindness, love. For if you possess these qualities in increasing measure; they will keep you from being ineffective and unproductive in your knowledge of our Lord Jesus Christ. -2 Peter 1:5-8

Consider it pure joy, my brothers, whenever you face trials of many kinds, because you know that the testing of your faith develops perseverance. Perseverance must finish its work so that you may be complete, not lacking anything. -James 1:2-4 Against all hope, Abraham in hope believed and so became the father of many nations, just as it had been said to him, "So shall your offspring be." Without weakening in his faith, he faced the fact that his body was good as dead. Yet he did not waver through unbelief regarding the promise of God, but was strengthened in faith and gave glory to God being fully persuaded that God had power to do what he promised. -Romans 4:18-20

Now faith is being sure of what we hope for and certain of what we do not see. This is what the ancients were commended for. -Hebrews 11:1 By faith Abel offered to God a better sacrifice than Cain did. By faith he was commended as a righteous man, when God spoke well of his offerings. And by faith he still speaks, even though he is dead. By faith Enoch was taken from this life, so that he did not experience death; he could not be found, because God had taken him away. For before he was taken, he was commended as one who pleased God. And without faith it is impossible to please God, because anyone that comes to him must believe that he exists and that he rewards those who earnestly seek him. By faith Noah, when warned about things not yet seen, in holy fear built an ark to save his family. By his faith he condemned the world and became heir of righteousness that comes by faith. By faith Abraham, when called to go to a place he would later receive as his inheritance, obeyed and went, even though he did not know where he was going. By faith he made his home in the Promised Land like a stranger in a foreign country; he lived in tents, as did Isaac and

Jacob, who were heirs of him with the same promise. -Hebrews 11:4-9

By faith Abraham, even though he was past age and Sarah herself was barren, was enabled to become a father because he considered him faithful who had made the promise. -Hebrews 11:11   By faith Abraham, when God tested him, offered Isaac as a sacrifice. He who had received the promises was about to sacrifice his one and only son, even though God had said to him, "it is through Isaac that your offspring will be reckoned." -Hebrews 11:17-18   By faith Isaac blessed Jacob and Esau in regard to their future. By faith Jacob, when he was dying, blessed each of Joseph's sons and worshiped as he leaned on the top of his staff. By faith Joseph, when his end was near, spoke about the exodus of the Israelites from Egypt and gave instructions about his bones. By faith Moses, when he had grown up, refused to be known as the son of pharaoh's daughter. He chose to be mistreated along with the people of God rather than to enjoy the pleasures of sin for a short time. -Hebrews 11:20-22, 24- 25

By Faith he left Egypt, not fearing the king's anger; he persevered because he saw him who is invisible. By faith he kept the Passover and the sprinkling of blood, so that the destroyer of the firstborn would not touch the firstborn of Israel. By faith people passed through the Red Sea as on dry land; but when the Egyptians tried to do so, they were drowned. By faith the walls of Jericho fell, after the people had marched around them for seven days. By faith the prostitute Rahab, because she welcomed the spies, was not killed with those who were disobedient. And what more shall I say? I do not have time to tell about Gideon, Barak, Samson and Jepthah, David and Samuel and the prophets, who through faith conquered kingdoms, administered justice, and gained what was promised; who shut the mouths of lions, quenched the fury of the flames, and escaped the edge of the sword; whose weakness was turned to strength; and who became powerful in battle and routed foreign armies. -Hebrews 11:27-34

Questions for Reflection and Discussion

1. On a scale of 1 to 10 how much do you trust God with the direction and wellbeing of your life?

2. What are some things that you could do to strengthen your faith in God?

3. What layer of faith do you personally struggle with and why?

4. In what ways can you strengthen the layer of faith that you struggle with the most?

CHAPTER 4

CHOSEN ONES

A lot of people struggle with the topic of being chosen or if they are good enough to have God love them. A lot of people use the fact that they are not good enough as an excuse to try to and not have a relationship with the Lord. There are some people out there who truly feel that because of all the things they have done they aren't good enough for God to accept, but we will get to those types of people in a moment. Back to the first group, the reason a lot of people say that they are not chosen is because it is an excuse. It is an excuse that they use because of the fear that they have inside them. They know that in order to have a relationship with the Lord, it is going to take a lot of hard work and a lot of effort and time on their behalf.

Now here's where the fear comes into place. You see, these people already know that the life they are living is wrong or that they really should be closer to God, and they may feel like God is trying to draw them in. That is when the fear will kick in and they will start asking themselves questions like, "what if I really do get committed and really put all my effort into this and I get disappointed, then what? After all that seeking out, putting that kind of hope into something and then it's nothing. I don't really think I can handle that kind of risk, that kind of disappointment in knowing that all along there really is no hope for me in my life. So if I never really seek God out in my life then I won't have to be disappointed and I can leave that part of my life void for now or search for it later, because I am not ready for that."

You see, that is the biggest lie that the devil could ever put in front of you, to believe that your Creator could ever disappoint you. The devil wants you to postpone the inevitable so that he can keep you from doing what God's will is for your life. That whole ploy is just one of his many tactics. What you need to realize is the truth. The truth of the matter is this: the God of the universe is your Creator; if He did not have faith in you as His creation then what would be the point in Him creating you. He created you for a purpose; that purpose is intended for His glory to show how great of a God He is in by what He created.

So, in this situation, if this is what you're struggling with and this is the reason that you have not committed to God yet, you need to realize God made you. He made you with a purpose in mind; the only way for you to know and achieve that purpose is by getting to know Him, He is the source of your existence. Your purpose isn't imprinted in you so that magically you will know what you need to do in life. You didn't come with a set of instructions when you were born explaining what you are to become. That is the whole point in why you have parents, so they can mold you and shape you into the person you need to be. You see, God loves you very much and because He created you He desires for you to have that relationship with Him. That way He can show you and guide you in what is best for you and your life.

The second biggest lie that the devil can throw at you is that you're not good enough, nor will you ever be good enough or you'll never be perfect so what's the point. What you have to realize is that God does not look at us like humans do. We could do something terribly wrong like kill someone or hurt someone, or just be a down right rotten person who does a lot of bad things for their own personal gain.

Now the world may look at these people and judge them as not being worthy. That's people, that's not God.

The devil will try to use this tool once again to delay what he doesn't want to happen and that is for you to have a relationship with your Father in Heaven. You have to understand because God is your heavenly Father and He is your Creator; He designed you. He created how you act, how you think, how you react, how you use your emotions, how your spirit inside you works and deals with things. So if you have a broken heart and a broken spirit; only the manufacturer knows how to repair it because He designed it, and He will fix those things too. All the hurt and pain that you have dealt with in life, He can fix so that you can be free of all that guilt and burden that can weigh you down on a daily basis.

Now, when it comes to this situation there is only one thing that you have to tell yourself and that is this: you're not perfect, you never were perfect and you never will be perfect, and that's OK. You see, if God was looking for people that were totally perfect and that never made mistakes He would have made a perfect world that could never have sin. The reason why God made the world like He did was because you can't get any joy when you force someone to be with you, or if you force them to love you. God made the world in a way so that it would come to Him naturally. He set up the Garden of Eden knowing that man was going to sin and disobey Him.

That's the reason why He sent His son to die on the cross, so that all mankind could still have the choice to seek Him out if we desired to. So you can't use the excuse you're not good enough or why would He like you? Because He knew you would sin and make bad choices but He still made you; and the offer to have a relationship is still on the table. Nothing can separate you from the love of God.

Remember this: everyone here on this earth has been given a choice. Choose to accept God and follow His ways or don't choose God. It really is as simple as that. Some people have a hard time accepting other people where they are in their station of life, but God can, and He wants to bring them to a higher station in their walk with Him. Even if you are someone who generally does good things and lives a decent life but just never made the commitment, God is ready to accept all of you, right where you are, at this moment.

Wisdom from God's Heart

"Here I am! I stand at the door and knock. If anyone hears my voice and opens the door, I will come in and dine with him, and he with me. To him who overcomes, I will give the right to sit with me on my throne, just as I overcame and sat down with my Father on his throne." -Revelation 3:20-21 The Spirit and the bride say, "Come!" And let him who hears say, "Come!" Whoever is thirsty, let him come: and whoever wishes, let him take the free gift of the water of life. -Revelation 22:17 "It is not the healthy who need a doctor, but the sick. But go and learn what this means: 'I desire mercy, not sacrifice.' For I have not come to call the righteous, but sinners." -Matthew 9:12-13 "Come to me, all you who are weary and burdened, and I will give you rest. Take my yoke upon you and learn from me, for I am gentle and humble in heart, and you will find rest for your souls. For my yoke is easy and my burden is light." -Matthew 11:28-30

As has just been said: "Today, if you hear his voice, do not harden your hearts as you did in the rebellion." -Hebrews 3:15 The promise is for you and your children and for all who are far off, for all whom the Lord God will call. -Acts 2:39 The Lord has made his salvation known and revealed his righteousness to the nations. He has remembered his love and his faithfulness to the house of Israel; all the ends of the earth have seen the salvation of our God. -Psalm 98:2-3

For Christ died for sins once for all. The righteous for the unrighteous, to bring you to God. He was put to death in the body but made alive by the spirit. -1 Peter 3:18 For the grace of God that brings salvation has appeared to all men! -Titus 2:11 "For I take no pleasure in the death of anyone, declares the sovereign Lord. Repent and live!" -Ezekiel 18:32 He is patient with you, not wanting anyone to perish, but everyone to come to repentance. -2 Peter 3:9 This is good, and pleases God our savior, who wants all men to be saved and to come to a knowledge of truth! -1 Timothy 2:3-4

The Lord is gracious and compassionate, slow to anger and rich in love. The Lord is good to all; he has compassion on all he has made. -Psalm 145:8-9   He is before all things, and in him all things hold together. -Colossians 1:17   The heavens declare the glory of God; the skies proclaim the work of his hands. Day after day they pour forth speech; night after night they display knowledge. There is no speech, or language where their voice is not heard. Their voice goes out into all the earth, their words to the ends of the world. -Psalm 19:1-4

A person can do nothing better than to eat and drink and find satisfaction in his work. This too, I see, is from the hand of God, for without him, who can eat or find enjoyment? -Ecclesiastes 2:24-25 In the past, he let all nations go their own way. Yet he has not left himself without testimony: He has shown kindness by giving you rain from heaven and crops in their seasons; he provides you with plenty of food and fills your hearts with joy. -Acts 14:16-17

For as high as the heavens are above the earth, so great is his love for those who fear him; as far as the east is from the west, so far has he removed our transgressions from us. As a father has compassion on his children, so the Lord has compassion on those who fear him. -Psalm 103:11-13   You are forgiving and good, O Lord, abounding in love to all who call on you. -Psalm 86:5   For the earth will be filled with the knowledge of the glory of the Lord as waters cover the sea. -Habakkuk 2:14

All the ways of the Lord are loving and faithful for those who keep the demands of his covenant. -Psalm 25:10   But now revealed and made known through the prophetic writings by the command of the eternal God, so that all nations might believe and obey him, to the only wise God be glory forever through Jesus Christ! Amen. -Romans 16:26-27   For those God foreknew he also predestined to be conformed to the likeness of his son.   -Romans 8:29

Since what may be known about God is plain to them, because God has made it plain to them. For since the creation of the world God's invisible qualities, his eternal power and divine nature, have been clearly seen, being understood from what has been made, so that men are without excuse. -Romans 1:19-20   For he chose us in him before the creation of the world to be holy and blameless in his sight. For God did not call us to be impure, but to live a holy life. -Ephesians 1:4, 1 Thessalonians 4:7

In his pride the wicked does not seek him; in all his thoughts there is no room for God! -Psalm 10:4 They perish because they refused to love the truth and to be saved! -2 Thessalonians 2:10 Furthermore, since they did not think it worthwhile to retain the knowledge of God, he gave them over to a depraved mind, to do what ought not to be done. -Romans 1:28 Even though I was once a blasphemer and a persecutor and a violent man, I was shown mercy because I acted in ignorance and unbelief. The grace of our Lord was poured out on me abundantly, along with the faith and love that are in Christ Jesus. Here is a trustworthy saying that deserves full acceptance: Christ Jesus came into the world to save sinners, of whom I am the worst. -1 Timothy 1:13-15

For I am not ashamed of the gospel, because it is the power of God that brings salvation to everyone who believes: first to the Jew, then to the Gentile. For in the gospel the righteousness of God is revealed, a righteousness that is by faith from first to last, just as it is written: "The righteous will live by faith." The wrath of God is being revealed from heaven against all the godlessness and wickedness of people, who suppress the truth by their wickedness. -Romans 1:16-18

In putting everything under him, God left nothing that is not subject to him. Yet at present we do not see everything subject to him. But we see Jesus, who was made lower than the angels for a little while, now crowned with glory and honor because he suffered death, so that by the grace of God he might taste death for everyone. In bringing many sons to glory, it was fitting that God, for whom and through whom everything exists, should make the author of their salvation perfect through suffering. -Hebrews 2:8-10

For all have sinned and fall short of the glory of God, and are justified freely by his grace through the redemption that came by Christ Jesus. God presented him as a sacrifice of atonement, through faith in his Blood! -Romans 3:23-25 For God does not show favoritism! -Romans 2:11 The scripture foresaw that God would justify the gentiles by faith, and announced the gospel in advance to

Abraham; "All nations will be blessed through you." So that those who have faith are blessed along with Abraham, the man of faith. -Galatians 3:8-9

"I tell you the truth, if anyone keeps my word, he will never see death!" -John 8:51 Christ became the source of eternal salvation for all who obey him. -Hebrews 5:9 Seek the Lord while he may be found; call on him while he is near! -Isaiah 55:6 "You will seek me and find me when you seek me with all your heart." -Jeremiah 29:13 Those who seek the Lord lack no good thing! -Psalm 34:10

Whenever anyone turns to the Lord, the veil is taken away. Now the Lord is the spirit, and where the spirit of the Lord is, there is freedom. And we, who with unveiled faces all reflect the Lord's glory, are being transformed into his likeness with ever-increasing glory, which comes from the Lord, who is spirit. -2 Corinthians 3:16-18

"For my fathers will is that everyone who looks to the son and believes in him shall have eternal life, and I will raise him up at the last day." -John 6:40

From one man he made every nation of men that they should inhabit the whole earth; and he determined the times set for them and the exact places where they should live. God did this so that men would seek him and perhaps reach out for him and find him, though he is not far from each one of us! -Acts 17:26-27 "All that the father gives me will come to me, and whoever comes to me I will never drive away!" -John 6:37

Then those who feared the Lord talked with each other, and the Lord listened and heard. A scroll of remembrance was written in his presence concerning those who feared the Lord and honored his name. "They will be mine," says the Lord Almighty, "In the day when I make up my treasured possession. I will spare them, just as a father has compassion and spares his son who serves him. And you will again see the distinction between the righteous and the wicked, between those who serve God and those who do not." -Malachi 3:16-18

For you created my inmost being; you knit me together in my mother's womb. I praise you because I am fearfully and wonderfully made; your works are wonderful, I know that full well. My frame was not hidden from you when I was made in the secret place, when I was woven together in the depths of the earth. -Psalm 139:13-15 "Behold, I am coming soon! My reward is with me, and I will give to everyone according to what he has done." -Revelation 22:12

Questions for Reflection and Discussion

1. What are some sin issues in a person's life that would cause them to struggle with the idea of God accepting them?

2. Was there ever a moment in your life when you may have doubted being good enough to accept the love that God has for you? If so, how did you overcome that moment so your doubt was eliminated?

3. As Christians what are some ways that we can show one another the reassurance of God's love?

4. As a Christian what are some ways that we can show the world that God desires a relationship with them as well?

CHAPTER FIVE

GOD'S HEART

I guess you could say that this chapter of the book is the heart and soul of the whole book itself. I truly believe that this chapter is what the core of Christianity should be. In my heart of hearts I believe that in order to be able to make a difference for the Lord, you truly have to have the desire to want to serve Him, to fulfill your purpose in bringing Him glory. These are the most important things as Christians to remember and focus on; because it is the Heart of God. These scriptures are a vital key to understanding and being able to please Him. These are the matters that are most important to Him. I believe in your Christian walk there are two things that should be most important for you to do in order to be completely successful at being a Christian.

The first thing is to completely surrender your life to Christ, to establish a strong relationship with Him, to love Him and worship Him in all that you do and in that, you will bring glory to Him. With that being said, that isn't something that can take place in a day, but the more you focus on loving Him, the more you focus on serving Him and you keep focused on that on a daily basis then that love and faithfulness will blossom into a strong foundation that cannot be broken.

The second thing is to give up yourself as an offering to God. The best way that you can wholeheartedly serve God is to help those who are in need. I have been a Christian for quite some time, and the one thing that I am truly starting to learn and comprehend is that this life of mine, it's not about me. This life that I have, and this life that I live, was never mine to begin with. We never had the choice to sign up for this life. We never had the choice to say yes, I would like to experience these things in life, these joys, pains, blessings and sufferings. So if we never had the choice or the chance to volunteer then it was never about us any ways. It was always and will always be about God. God has a plan and we are the tools that He needs to use to get things done. If you look at the big picture, it is way bigger than what we are or what we can ever really imagine. I think that is why the biggest problem people have today, as followers of Christ, is that they only want to commit to the first half and go to church and have a devotional or two and call that a relationship. It's as if they really feel that they have a choice in the matter, but really it is not about them at all. That is why I feel that understanding this truth and really taking this truth to heart can make a difference to changing the world and starting a revival on a global scale. This is God's heart, this is most important to Him.

People are always saying, "I want to know God on a deeper level." I can definitely say that a huge way you can really get to know God is by spending time helping others. The funny thing is, in the Word, God promises over and over how He will bless you and help you in your life if you just help others.

Today, we live in a world with over 7 billion people; there really is no excuse not to help someone. You might say, "Well I can't just give up my job and go to Africa or another country to help out all these poor people." Maybe not, but I would bet that if you sat and thought hard enough, you could think of someone right now that you know of who needs your help. I am also willing to say, and maybe this is stretching just a little, that just maybe God has already been convicting you that you should help them.

If you really want to know what God's heart is; it's simple, it's His people, and it's His creation. Remember, He created everyone and if He is our father than that makes us all brothers and sisters. God's desire for us as a whole world is that we get taken care of. It's our responsibility to look out for one another. Think about it, if every person gave 1 dollar and put it toward world hunger, that's seven billion dollars. With that amount we could stop world hunger.

That is just with one dollar. You see, it is time for us as Christians to stop thinking about just ourselves and to take the lead and start taking care of the world. We are the only hope that they have. If we don't do it then nobody else will.

Wisdom from God's Heart

"He did what was right and just, so all went well with him! He defended the cause of the poor and needy, and so all went well. Is that not what it means to know me? Declares the Lord!" -Jeremiah 22:15-16 "Only if you carefully obey the voice of the Lord your God to observe with care all these commandments which I command you today. For the Lord your God will bless you just as He promised you; you shall lend to many nations, but you shall not borrow; you shall reign over many nations but they shall not reign over you. If there is among you a poor man of your brethren, within any of the gates in your land which the Lord your God is giving you, you shall not harden your heart nor shut your hand from your poor brother, but you shall open your hand wide to him and willingly lend him sufficient for his need, whatever he needs. Beware lest there be a wicked thought in your heart, saying, 'The seventh year, the year of release, is at hand,' and your eye be evil against your poor brother and you give him nothing, and he cry out to the Lord against you, and it became sin among you. You shall surely give to him, and your heart should not be grieved when you give to him, because for this thing the Lord your God will bless you in all your works and in all to which you put your hand. For the poor will never cease from the land; therefore I command you, saying, 'You shall open your hand wide to your brother, to your poor and your needy, in your land." -Deuteronomy 15:5-11

He who gives to the poor will lack nothing, be he who closes his eyes to them receives many curses. -Proverbs 28:27 If anyone does not provide for his relatives, and especially for his immediate family, he has denied the faith and is worse than an unbeliever. -1 Timothy 5:8 A poor man is shunned by all his relatives, how much more do his friends avoid him! Though he pursues them with pleading, they are nowhere to be found. -Proverbs 19:7   The poor are shunned even by their neighbors, but the rich have many friends. He who despises his neighbor sins, but blessed is he who is kind to the needy! -Proverbs 14:20-21 A generous man will himself be blessed, for he shares his food with the poor. -Proverbs 22:9   The righteous care about justice for the poor, but the wicked have no such concern. -Proverbs 29:7   Blessed are those who fear the LORD, who find great delight in his commands. Good will come to those who are generous and lend freely, who conduct their affairs with justice. Surely the righteous will never be shaken; they will be remembered forever. They will have no fear of bad news; their hearts are steadfast, trusting in the LORD. They have freely scattered their gifts to the poor, their righteousness endures forever; their horn will be lifted high in honor. -Psalm 112:1, 5-7, 9   He who is kind to the poor lends to the Lord, and he will reward him for what he has done! -Proverbs 19:17 He who oppresses the poor shows contempt for their maker! But whoever is kind to the needy honors God! -Proverbs 14:31

He who mocks the poor shows contempt for their maker; whoever gloats over disaster will not go unpunished. -Proverbs 17:5   If a man shuts his ears to the cry of the poor, he too will cry out and not be answered! -Proverbs 21:13   Do not withhold good from those who deserve it, when it is in your power to act. Do not say to your neighbor, "Come back tomorrow and I'll give it to you." When you already have it with you. -Proverbs 3:27-28   "In everything, do unto others what you would have them do unto you!" -Matthew 7:12   Be devoted to one another in brotherly love. Honor one another above yourself! - Romans 12:10   Nobody should seek his own good, but the good of others. -1 Corinthians 10:24

"When you give a luncheon or dinner, do not invite your friends, your brothers or sisters, your relatives, or your rich neighbors; if you do, they may invite you back and so you will be repaid. But when you give a banquet, invite the poor, the crippled, the lame, the blind, and you will be blessed. Although they cannot repay you, you will be repaid at the resurrection of the righteous." - Luke 14:12-14

Remember this: Whoever sows sparingly will also reap sparingly, and whoever sows generously will also reap generously. Each of you should give what you have decided in your heart to give, not reluctantly or under compulsion, for God loves a cheerful giver. And God is able to bless you abundantly, so that in all things at all times, having all that you need, you will abound in every good work. As it is written: "They have freely scattered their gifts to the poor; their righteousness endures forever." -2 Corinthians 9:6-9

We who are strong ought to bear with the failings of the weak and not to please ourselves. Each of us should please our neighbors for their good, to build them up. For even Christ did not please himself but, as it is written: "The insults of those who insult you have fallen on me." For everything that was written in the past was written to teach us, so that through the endurance taught in the Scriptures and the encouragement they provide we might have hope. Accept one another, then, just as Christ accepted you, in order to bring praise to God. -Romans 15:1-4, 7

"Do not be afraid, little flock, for your Father has been pleased to give you the kingdom. Sell your possessions and give to the poor. Provide purses for yourselves that will not wear out, a treasure in heaven that will never fail, where no thief comes near and no moth destroys. -Luke 12:32-33 "I tell you the truth, whatever you did for the least of these brothers of mine, you did for me!" -Matt 25:40 Share with God's people who are in need. Practice hospitality. -Romans 12:13 Offer hospitality to one another without grumbling. Each one should use whatever gift he has received to serve others, faithfully administering God's grace in various forms. -1 Peter 4:9-10

We urge you, brothers and sisters, warn those who are idle and disruptive, encourage the disheartened, help the weak, be patient with everyone. Make sure that nobody pays back wrong for wrong, but always strive to do what is good for each other and for everyone else. -1 Thessalonians 5:14-15 "Give to the one who asks you, and do not turn away from the one who wants to borrow from you." -Matthew 5:42 "I tell you, love your enemies and pray for those who persecute you, that you may be sons of your father in heaven." -Matthew 5:44-45 "If your enemy is hungry, feed him; if he is thirsty, give him something to drink. In doing this, you will heap burning coals on his head." Do not be overcome by evil, but overcome evil with good. -Romans 12: 20-21

Do nothing out of selfish ambition or vain conceit. Rather, in humility value others above yourselves, not looking to your own interests but each of you to the interests of the others. -Philippians 2:3-4 For we are God's workmanship, created in Christ Jesus to do good works, which God has prepared in advance for us to do. -Ephesians 2:10 Carry each other's burdens, and in this way you will fulfill the law of Christ. If anyone thinks he is something when he is nothing, he deceives himself. Each one should test his own actions. Then he can take pride in himself, without comparing himself to somebody else, for each one should carry his own load. -Galatians 6:2-5

If anyone has material possessions and sees his brother in need but has no pity on him, how can the love of God be in him? Dear children, let us not love with words or tongue but with actions and in truth. -1 John 3:17-18 What good is it, my brothers, if a man claims to have faith but has no deeds? Can such faith save him? Suppose a brother or sister is without clothes and daily food. If one of you says to him "Go, I wish you well; keep warm and well fed," but does nothing about his physical needs, what good is it? In the same way, faith by itself, if it is not accompanied by action, is dead. -James 2:14-17

Who is the wise and understanding among you? Let him show it by his good life, by deeds done in the humility that comes from wisdom. -James 3:13 Someone will say, "You have faith; I have deeds." Show me your faith without deeds, and I will show you my faith by what I do! -James 2:18 After an absence of several years, I came to Jerusalem to bring my people gifts for the poor and to present offerings. -Acts 24:17

All they asked was that we should continue to remember the poor, the very thing I was eager to do! -Galatians 2:10 You yourselves know that these hands of mine have supplied my own needs and the needs of my companions. In everything I did, I showed you this kind of hard work we must help the weak, remembering the words the Lord Jesus himself said: "It is more blessed to give than to receive." -Acts 20:34-35

Anyone, then, who knows the good he ought to do and doesn't do it, sins. -James 4:17 Do not merely listen to the word, and so deceive yourselves. Do what it says. Anyone who listens to the word but does not do what it says is like a man who looks at his face in the mirror and, after looking at himself, goes away and immediately forgets what he looks like. But the man who looks intently into the perfect law that gives freedom, and continues to do this, not forgetting what he has heard, but doing it he will be blessed in what he does. -James 1:22-25

Religion that God our father accepts as pure and faultless is this: to look after orphans and widows in their distress and to keep oneself from being polluted by the world. -James 1:27 When you spread out your hands in prayer, I will hide my eyes from you; even if you offer many prayers, I will not listen. Your hands are full of blood; wash and make yourselves clean. Take your evil deeds out of my sight! Stop doing wrong. Learn to do right! Seek justice, encourage the oppressed. Defend the cause of the fatherless, plead the case of the widow. - Isaiah 1:15-17

I charge you in the sight of God and Christ Jesus and the elect angels. Keep these instructions without partiality, and do nothing out of favoritism. -1 Timothy 5:21 And do not forget to do good and to share with others, for with such sacrifices God is pleased. -Hebrews 13:16 To those who by persistence in doing good seek glory, honor and immortality, he will give eternal life! -Romans 2:7 We know that we have passed from death to life, because we love our brothers. Anyone who does not love remains in death. -1 John 3:14

We pray that you may live a life worthy of the Lord and may please him in every way: bearing fruit in every good work, growing in the knowledge of God. -Colossians 1:10 "Do not store up for yourselves treasures on earth, where moth and rust destroy, and where thieves break in and steal. But store up for yourselves treasures in heaven, where moth and rust do not destroy, and where thieves do not break in and steal." -Matthew 6:19-20

Questions for Reflection and Discussion

1. Can you think of a time in your life when you had done a random act of kindness? Explain what it was.

2. How did you feel after your kindness was displayed?

3. Are there any people in your life that you could help out in some small way? If so, name them.

4. List the ways that you may be able to help these people that you know?

5. List some small ways that you as a church may be able to help others. Discuss which ones you would like to bring into effect.

CHAPTER SIX

GOD'S WILL

This can be the toughest question that we will ever try to figure out in our life. What is God's will for my life? Where do I go from here? You know it would be so nice if God were to magically show up like a genie and POOF! Here is the rest of your life on a nice little platter, everything I want you to do.

Unfortunately that is not how free will works, considering the fact that God wants us to seek Him out. I don't know about you, but one of my greatest fears is that when I die and go to heaven and I talk to God, I don't want Him to be like, "Ok.... here was everything that I had planned for you.... And..... Here is what you did." I just don't want to be so disappointed and let Him down.

There are so many questions to ask about God's will. How do I find it? Where do I find it? Does that mean I have to go into ministry full time? Do I have to become a pastor or a missionary? Do I have to leave the country? Do I work a regular job in life like everyone else? What is my purpose for God?

I can tell you this: We were all created with different talents and abilities. God wants to use those talents and abilities for His glory. Now some of you might be thinking, well, I don't have any special talents or abilities. Trust me, you do. I feel the same way. There are times when you might feel that you don't have a lot to offer in the talent department, but your willingness to serve can be a very special talent and ability.

I guess two of the questions you have to ask yourself is this: "What am I willing to give up as I'm seeking out God's will for my life, and what am I willing to do for Him in order to serve Him as best as I possibly can?" We all give our lives to the Lord at a certain point in our life. Depending on where we are at in that specific time of our life will depict the types of questions we may be asking God about what His will for our life is. Some of you who are older and have lived life may be thinking, "I'm older now, I'm not as young as I used to be, how do I determine what God's will is for my life?"

Some of you may be asking the question, "I have a full time job and a family to look after, how do I find out what God's will is?" Some of you may be younger and don't know where to turn to. Do I go to college or Bible school? Or do I just get a regular job and work like everyone else.

Here is the cool thing about this chapter. Although you may not know all the specifics for what God's will is for your life. I can tell you this; you'll never be able to completely figure out every little detail, until you have lived your whole life and your standing before God. The Bible gives you enough information so that you know what the general idea is of how God wants you to live your life (His will). Now, as life happens, you may discover specific pieces of what God's will is for your life.

The cool thing is if you live out what His will is, through these scriptures, it doesn't really matter what you're position in life is, you will know that God's is directing in every aspect of your life. Just remember this, as long as you're seeking Him out and trusting in Him, He will guide your steps.

Wisdom from God's Heart

Religion that God our Father accepts as pure and faultless is this: to look after orphans and widows in their distress and to keep oneself from being polluted by the world. -James 1:27 My son, pay attention to what I say; listen closely to my words. Do not let them out of your sight, keep them within your heart; for they are life to those who find it and health to all their flesh. -Proverbs 4:20-22 All Scripture is God-breathed and is useful for teaching, rebuking, correcting and training in righteousness, so that the man of God may be thoroughly equipped for every good work. -2 Timothy 3:16-17

If you accept my words and store up my commands within you, turning your ear to wisdom and apply your heart to understanding. Indeed, if you call out for insight and cry aloud for understanding, and if you look for it as for silver and search for it as for hidden treasure, then you will understand the fear of the Lord and find the knowledge of God. For the Lord gives wisdom; from his mouth come knowledge and understanding. -Proverbs 2:1-6

"Love the Lord your God with all your heart and with all your soul and with all your mind and with all your strength." The second is this: 'Love your neighbor as yourself.' There is no commandment greater than these." -Mark 12:30-31 All the Law and the Prophets hang on these two commandments." -Matthew 22:40 So in everything, do to others what you would have them do to you, for this sums up the Law and the Prophets. -Matthew 7:12

"This is what the LORD Almighty says: 'Administer true justice; show mercy and compassion to one another. Do not oppress the widow or the fatherless, the alien or the poor. In your hearts do not think evil of each other.' -Zechariah 7:8-10 Set the oppressed free and break every yoke. Is it not to share your food with the hungry and to provide the poor wanderer with shelter? When you see the naked, to clothe them, and not to turn away from your own flesh and blood? Then your light will break forth like the dawn, and your healing will quickly appear; then your righteousness will go before you, and the glory of the LORD will be your rear guard. Then you will call, and the LORD will answer; you will cry for help, and he will say: Here am I. "If you do away with the yoke of oppression, with the pointing finger and malicious talk, and if you spend yourselves in behalf of the hungry and satisfy the needs of the oppressed, then your light will rise in the darkness, and your night will become like the noonday. The LORD will guide you always; he will satisfy your needs in a sun-scorched land and will strengthen your frame. You will be like a well-watered garden, like a spring whose waters never fail. Then you will find your joy in the LORD, and I will cause you to ride in triumph on the heights of the land." For the mouth of the LORD has spoken. -Isaiah 58:6-11, 14

Blessed are all who fear the LORD, who walk in obedience to him. You will eat the fruit of your labor; blessings and prosperity will be yours. -Psalm 128:1-2 Blessed are those whose ways are blameless, who walk according to the law of the LORD. Blessed are those who keep his statutes and seek him with all their heart. -Psalm 119:1-2 Seek the LORD while he may be found; call on him while he is near. -Isaiah 55:6

"If anyone would come after me, he must deny himself and take up his cross and follow me. For whoever wants to save his life will lose it, but whoever loses his life for me will find it." -Matthew 16:24-25 "Whoever serves me must follow me; and where I am, my servant also will be. My Father will honor the one who serves me." -John 12:26 "For the Son of Man is going to come in his Father's glory with his angels, and then he will reward each person according to what he has done." -Matthew 16:27

"Not everyone who says to me, 'Lord, Lord,' will enter the kingdom of heaven, but only the one who does the will of my Father in heaven." -Matthew 7:21 "For I have come down from heaven not to do my will but to do the will of him who sent me. And this is the will of him who sent me, that I shall lose none of all he has given me, but raise them up at the last day. For my Father's will is that everyone who looks to the Son and believes in him shall have eternal life, and I will raise him up at the last day." -John 6:38-40

"The one who sent me is with me; he has not left me alone, for I always do what pleases him." -John 8:29 "For the Son of Man did not come to be served, but to serve, and to give his life as a ransom for many." -Matthew 20:28 "My command is this: Love each other as I have loved you. Greater love has no one than this: that he lay down his life for his friends. You are my friends if you do what I command!" -John 15:12-14 "I am the vine; you are the branches. If a man remains in me and I in him, he will bear much fruit; apart from me you can do nothing. If anyone does not remain in me, he is like a branch that is thrown away and withers; such branches are picked up, thrown into the fire and burned. If you remain in me and my words remain in you, ask whatever you wish, and it will be done for you. This is to my Father's glory, that you bear much fruit, showing yourselves to be my disciples." -John 15:5-8

"Do not work for food that spoils, but for food that endures to eternal life, which the Son of Man will give you. For on him God the Father has placed his seal of approval." -John 6:27 "If you hold to my teaching, you are really my disciples. Then you will know the truth, and the truth will set you free." -John 8:31-32 "If you obey my commands, you will remain in my love, just as I have obeyed my Father's commands and remain in his love." -John 15:10

Jesus Christ died for all, that those who live should no longer live for themselves but for him who died for them and was raised again. -2 Corinthians 5:15 In him we have redemption through his blood, the forgiveness of sins, in accordance with the riches of God's grace that he lavished on us. With all wisdom and understanding, he made known to us the mystery of his will according to his good pleasure, which he purposed in Christ, to be put into effect when the times reach their fulfillment, to bring unity to all things in heaven and on earth together under one head, even Christ. -Ephesians 1:7-10

Therefore, I urge you, brothers in view of God's mercy, to offer your bodies as a living sacrifice, holy and pleasing to God. This is spiritual act of worship. Do not conform any longer to the pattern of this world, but be transformed by the renewing of your mind. Then you will be able to test and approve what God's will is, his good, pleasing and perfect will. -Romans 12:1-2 I urge you, as aliens and strangers in the world, to abstain from sinful desires, which wage war against your souls. Live such good lives among the pagans that, though they accuse you of doing wrong, they may see your good deeds and glorify God on the day he visits us. -1 Peter 2:11-12

Do not love the world or anything in the world. If anyone loves the world, love for the Father is not in them. For everything in the world, the cravings of sinful man, the lust of his eyes and the boasting of what he has and does, comes not from the Father but from the world. The world and its desires pass away, but the man who does the will of God lives forever. -1 John 2:15-17

Be very careful, then, how you live, not as unwise but as wise, making the most of every opportunity, because the days are evil. Therefore do not be foolish, but understand what the Lord's will is. Do not get drunk on wine, which leads to debauchery. Instead, be filled with the Spirit, speaking to one another with psalms, hymns, and spiritual songs. Sing and make music in your heart to the Lord, always giving thanks to God the Father for everything, in the name of our Lord Jesus Christ. Submit to one another out of reverence for Christ. -Ephesians 5:15-21

Be joyful always; pray continually, give thanks in all circumstances; for this is God's will for you in Christ Jesus. Do not put out the spirits fire. Do not treat prophecy with contempt test everything. Hold on to the good. Avoid every kind of evil. -1 Thessalonians 5:16-22 We pray that you may live a life worthy of the Lord and please him in every way: bearing fruit in every good work, growing in the knowledge of God. -Colossians 1:10 I pray that you may be active in sharing your faith so that you will have a full understanding of every good thing we have in Christ. -Philemon 1:6

My purpose is that you may be encouraged in heart and united in love, so that they may have the full riches of complete understanding, in order that they may know the mystery of God, namely, Christ, in whom are hidden all the treasures of wisdom and knowledge. -Colossians 2:2-3 For we are God's workmanship, created in Christ Jesus to do good works, which God prepared in advance for us to do. -Ephesians 2:10

In Christ Jesus the only thing that counts is faith expressing itself through love. -Galatians 5:6 And this is love: that we walk in obedience to his commands. -2 John 1:6 So let us love one another, for love comes from God. Everyone who loves has been born of God and knows God. Whoever does not love does not know God, because God is love. -1 John 4:7-8 And this is his command: to believe in the name of his Son, Jesus Christ, and to love one another as he commanded us. Those who obey God's commands lives in him, and he in them. And this is how we know that he lives in us:

We know it by the Spirit he gave us. -1 John 3:23-24

We know that we have come to know him if we obey his commands. The man who says, "I know him," but does not do what he commands is a liar, and the truth is not in him. But if anyone obeys his word, God's love is truly made complete in him. This is how we know we are in him: Whoever claims to live in him must walk as Jesus did. -1 John 2:3-6 Through Jesus, therefore, let us continually offer to God a sacrifice of praise, the fruit of lips that confess his name. And do not forget to do good and to share with others, for with such sacrifices God is pleased. -Hebrews 13:15-16

So do not throw away your confidence; it will be richly rewarded. You need to persevere so that when you have done the will of God, you will receive what he has promised. -Hebrews 10:35-36 And God is able to make all grace abound to you, so that in all things at all times, having all that you need, you will abound in every good work. -2 Corinthians 9:8 To those who by persistence in doing good seek glory, honor and immortality, he will give eternal life. -Romans 2:7

Who is wise and understanding among you? Let him show it by his good life, by deeds done in the humility that comes from wisdom. -James 3:13 Now all has been heard; here is the conclusion of the matter: Fear God and keep his commandments, for this is the whole duty of man. For God will bring every deed into judgment, including every hidden thing, whether it is good or evil. -Ecclesiastes 12:13-14

"When the Son of Man comes in his glory, and all the angels with him, he will sit on his glorious throne. He will put the sheep on his right and the goats on his left. Then the King will say to those on his right, 'Come, you who are blessed by my Father; take your inheritance, the kingdom prepared for you since the creation of the world. For I was hungry and you gave me something to eat, I was thirsty and you gave me something to drink, I was a stranger and you invited me in, I needed clothes and you clothed me, I was sick and you looked after me, I was in prison and you came to visit me.' Then the righteous will answer him, 'Lord, when did we see you hungry and feed you, or thirsty and give you something to drink?

When did we see you a stranger and invite you in, or needing clothes and clothe you? When did we see you sick or in prison and go to visit you?' "The King will reply, 'Truly I tell you, whatever you did for one of the least of these brothers of mine, you did for me.' "Then he will say to those on his left, 'Depart from me, you who are cursed, into the eternal fire prepared for the devil and his angels. For I was hungry and you gave me nothing to eat, I was thirsty and you gave me nothing to drink, I was a stranger and you did not invite me in, I needed clothes and you did not clothe me, I was sick and in prison and you did not look after me.' "They also will answer, 'Lord, when did we see you hungry or thirsty or a stranger or needing clothes or sick or in prison, and did not help you?' "He will reply, 'Truly I tell you, whatever you did not do for one of the least of these, you did not do for me.' "Then they will go away to eternal punishment, but the righteous to eternal life." -Matthew 25:31, 33-46

"This is how it will be with anyone who stores up things for himself but is not rich toward God." -Luke 12:21 He who gives to the poor will lack nothing, but he who closes his eyes to them receives many curses. -Proverbs 28:27 Good will come to him who is generous and lend freely, who conducts his affairs with justice. Surely the righteous will never be shaken; A righteous man will be remembered forever. -Psalm 112:5-6

You know we have passed from death to life, because we love our brother. Anyone who does not love remains in death. -1 John 3:14 "Who then is the faithful and wise servant, whom the master has put in charge of the servants in his household to give them their food at the proper time? It will be good for that servant whose master finds him doing so when he returns. I tell you the truth, he will put him in charge of all his possessions." -Matthew 24:45-47

"The servant who knows the master's will and does not get ready or does not do what the master wants will be beaten with many blows. But the one who does not know and does things deserving punishment will be beaten with few blows." -Luke 12:47-48 If anyone, then, knows the good he ought to do and doesn't do it, sins. -James 4:17

Questions for Reflection and Discussion

1. What are some talents and abilities that you have that you could use for God's will in your life?

2. What are some situations that you personally have experienced in your life, maybe a hardship or trial or maybe even a tragedy, that has made you stronger as a person, something that you could help someone else get through who might need your help and guidance?

3. What are some instructions that God wants you to incorporate in your life that come from scripture that you may struggle with? (Example: love your enemy)

4. What are some things that you could do to overcome these struggles that you deal with?

Chapter Seven

Love

Love, it is one of the most amazing gifts that you can possess as a human being. There are so many ways that we can demonstrate this four-letter word. It has been said that love holds no bounds. Some of the stories you hear about what people have done in the name of love are incredible, the challenges and obstacles that people have faced and overcome, and the years of dedication and devotion that people have given to one another, just amazes me.

The sad thing is, in today's society, the world doesn't really know what true love is, they use the word love more like an adjective than they use it as a verb. For example, you might hear someone say, "Oh I love pizza!" or, "I love that new outfit they came out with at Forever 21." "I love that new song that came out by so and so." Really, is that what love is all about? Now, some of you are saying to yourself, "Give me a break, I know better than that, it's just an expression." OK, maybe you're right or maybe not. For example, let's take a look at some of the well-known people or celebrities. They are hooking up with one person, then in a couple of months they are with another.

A lot of times we will see a certain celebrity get married and then a couple of years later they get divorced. To them, and to society as a whole, this is no big deal, it's normal, it happens. The problem is there is no sense of commitment or devotion, they just pass it on and go with the next big thing. Isn't that kind of like saying I LOVE PIZZA! Sure you love pizza, but you're not eating it every day either are you. Now don't get me wrong, I don't have anything against pizza. I like to eat pizza just like everyone else, but in the same token, these people that our society looks up to, famous people who are icons in the world's eyes, are showing the same kind of love like you show pizza.

The divorce rate in America alone is 40 to 50 percent. So basically if you are married, you have a 50/50 shot of it working out. That sure sounds like winning odds doesn't it. The sad thing is we are talking about loving your spouse, the one you're supposed to be committed to for the rest of your life! That is only one type of love. We haven't even touched on the other side of love like the love for your fellow man.

So let's take the highest form of commitment that the world holds to the highest value, which is showing love to our spouse, which is supposed to be a sacred bond between a man, woman and God, and we give that a 50/50 success rate. Next, we go to something less sacred like loving one another, things like helping out your family or friends, helping out people who are poor. That has an even smaller successful commitment rating. So then how much is being put into a serious commitment of loving the Lord our God, someone we can't see, or touch?

So what can we do about this? How do we fix this so that our perception and the way we value love isn't so distorted and messed up? We need to go to the one who is the true illustrator of love, to the one who has loved deeper than anyone in this world could ever conceive, to the one who paid the ultimate price, the one who sacrificed more than anyone in the name of Love, Jesus Christ.

Wisdom from God's Heart

Love the Lord your God with all your heart all your soul and with all your strength. -Deuteronomy 6:5 The Lord your God will circumcise your hearts and the hearts of your descendants, so that you may love him with all your heart and with all your soul. -Deuteronomy 30:6 So if you faithfully obey the commands I am giving you today to love the Lord your God and serve him with all your heart and with all your soul. Then I will send rain on your land in its season both autumn and spring rains so that you may gather in your grain, new wine and oil. I will provide grass in the fields for your cattle, and you will eat and be satisfied. -Deuteronomy 11:13-15 For I command you today to love the Lord your God, to walk in his ways and to keep his commands decrees and laws; and then you will live and increase and the Lord your God will bless you in the land you are entering to possess. -Deuteronomy 30:16

Love the Lord, all his saints! The Lord preserves the faithful, but the proud he pays back in full. -Psalm 31:23 Let those who love the Lord hate evil, for he guards the lives of his faithful ones and delivers them from the hand of the wicked. -Psalm 97:10 "Because he loves me," Says the Lord I will rescue him; I will protect him, for he acknowledges my name. -Psalm 91:14 I love you, O Lord, my strength. The Lord is my rock my fortress and my deliverer; My God is my rock in whom I take refuge. He is my shield and the horn of my salvation, my stronghold. -Psalm 18:1-2 I love the Lord for he heard my voice; he heard my cry for mercy. Because he turned his ear to me, I will call on him as long as I live. -Psalm 116:1-2 But may all who seek you rejoice and be glad in you; may those who love your salvation always say, the Lord be exalted. -Psalm 40:16

Oh, how I love your law! I meditate on it all day long. -Psalm 119:97 I hate and abhor falsehood but I love your law. -Psalm 119:163 Turn to me and have mercy on me as you always do to those who love your name. -Psalm 119:132 Great peace have they who love your law and nothing can make them stumble. —Psalm 119:165 See how I love your precepts; preserve my life, O Lord, according to your love. -Psalm 119:159 I obey your statutes for I love them greatly. -Psalm 119:167 All the wicked you discord like dross; therefore I love your statutes. -Psalm 119:119 The Lord watches over all who love him, but all the wicked he will destroy. -Psalm 145:20

Do not forsake wisdom, and she will protect you; love her, and she will watch over you. -Proverbs 4:6 He who covers offense promotes love, but whoever repeats the matter separates close friends. -Proverbs 17:9 Hatred stirs up dissension, but love covers all wrongs. -Proverbs 10:12 The tongue has the power of life and death, and those who love it will eat its fruit. -Proverbs 18:21 He has showed you, O man, what is good. What does the Lord require of you? To act justly and to love mercy and to walk humbly with your God. -Micah 6:8 "Do not plot evil against your neighbor and do not love to swear falsely, I hate all this." Declares the Lord. -Zechariah 8:17

"You have heard that it was said 'Love you neighbor and hate your enemy.' But I tell you, love your enemies and pray for those who persecute you. If you love those who love you, what reward will you get? Are not even the tax collectors doing that?" -Matthew 5:43-44, 46 "If you love those who love you what credit is that to you? Even sinners love those who love them." -Luke 6:32

"But love your enemies, do good to them, without expecting to get anything back. Then your reward will be great. And you will be sons of the most high, because he is kind to the ungrateful and wicked." -Luke 6:35 "But I tell you who hear me; love your enemies, do good to those who hate you, bless those who curse you, pray for those who mistreat you." -Luke 6:27-28 "My command is this: Love each other as I have loved you. Greater love has no one than this: that he lay down his life for his friends. -John 15:12-13 "As the father has loved me, so I have loved you. Now remain in my love, if you obey my commands, you will remain in my love, just as I have obeyed my father's commands and remain in his love." -John 15:9-10

"If you love me, you will obey what I command." -John 14:15 "Whoever has my commands and obeys them, he is the one who loves me. He who loves me will be loved by my father, and I too will love him and show myself to him." -John 14:21 "If anyone loves me he will obey my teaching. My father will love him, and we will come and make our home with him." -John 14:23 "But the world must learn that I love the father and that I do exactly what my father has commanded me." -John 14:31 "Because of the increase of wickedness, the love of most will grow cold, but he who stands firm to the end will be saved." -Matthew 24:12-13 But God demonstrates his own love for us in this: while we were still sinners Christ died for us. -Romans 5:8

And we know that in all things God works for the good of those who love him, who have been called according to his purpose. -Romans 8:28 And hope does not disappoint us, because God has poured out his love into our hearts by the Holy Spirit, whom he has given us. -Romans 5:5 Who shall separate us from the love of Christ? Shall trouble or hardship or persecution or famine or nakedness or danger or sword? As it is written: "For your sake we face death all day long; we are considered as sheep to be slaughtered." No, in all these things we are more than conquerors through him who loved us. For I am convinced that neither death nor life, neither angles nor demons, neither the present nor the future, nor any powers, neither height nor depth, nor anything else in all creation, will be able to separate us from the love of God. That is in Christ Jesus our Lord. -Romans 8:35-39

However as it is written: "No eye has seen no ear has heard, no mind has conceived what God had prepared for those who love him. -1 Corinthians 2:9 But the man who loves God is known by God. -1 Corinthians 8:3 For in Christ Jesus neither circumcision nor uncircumcision has any value. The only thing that counts is faith expressing itself through love. -Galatians 5:6 For Christ's love compels us, because we are convinced that one died for all, and therefore all died. -2 Corinthians 5:14 I am not commanding you, but I want to test the sincerity of your love by comparing it with the earnestness of others. -2 Corinthians 8:8

Let no debt remain outstanding, except the continuing debt to love one another, for he who loves his fellow man has fulfilled the law. -Romans 13:8 Love does no harm to its neighbor therefore love is the fulfillment of the law. -Romans 13:10 Love must be sincere. Hate what is evil; cling to what is good. Be devoted to one another in brotherly love. Honor one another above yourselves. -Romans 12:9-10

You, my brothers were called to be free. But do not use your freedom to indulge the sinful nature; rather serve one another in love. -Galatians 5:13 For he chose us in him before the creation of the world to be holy and blameless in his sight. In love he predestined us to be adopted sons through Jesus Christ, in accordance with his pleasure and will to the praise of his glorious grace, which he has freely given us in the one he loves. -Ephesians 1:4-6

For the kingdom of God is not a matter of talk but of power.

Which do you prefer? Shall I come to you with a whip, or in love and with a gentle spirit? -1 Corinthians 4:20-21 Then we will no longer be infants, tossed back and forth by the waves, and blown here and there by every wind of teaching and by cunning and craftiness of men in their deceitful scheming. Instead, speaking the truth in love, we will in all things grow up into him who is the head, that is, Christ. From him the whole body joined and held together by every supporting ligament, grows and builds itself up in love, as each part does its work. -Ephesians 4:14-16

Be imitators of God, therefore, as dearly loved children and live a life of love, just as Christ loved us and gave himself up for us as a fragment offering and sacrifice to God. -Ephesians 5:1-2 So that Christ may dwell in your hearts through faith. And I pray that you being rooted and established in love, may have the power, together with all the saints, to grasp how wide and long and how high and deep is the love of Christ, and to know this love that surpasses knowledge that you may be filled to the measure of all the fullness of God. -Ephesians 3:17-19

Be completely humble and gentle; be patient with one another in love. -Ephesians 4:2 Peace to the brothers, and love with faith from God the Father and the Lord Jesus Christ. -Ephesians 6:23 Grace to all who love our Lord Jesus Christ with an undying love. -Ephesians 6:24 And this is my prayer: that your love may abound more and more in its knowledge and depth and insight, so that you may be pure and blameless until the day of Christ. -Philippians 1:9-10 May the Lord make your love increase and over flow for each other and for everyone else, just as ours does for you. -1 Thessalonians 3:12

Husbands, love your wives, just as Christ loved the church and gave himself up for her to make her holy, cleansing her by the washing with water through the word. And to present her to himself as a radiant church, without stain or wrinkle or any other blemish, but holy and blameless. In the same way, husbands ought to love their wives as their own bodies. He who loves his wife loves himself. After all, no one ever hates his own body, but he feeds and cares for it, just as Christ does for the church. For we are members of his body. -Ephesians 5:25-31

Now we ask you brothers to respect those who work hard among you, who admonish you. Hold them in the highest regard in love because of their work. Live in peace with each other. -1 Thessalonians 5:12-13 May the Lord direct your hearts into God's love and Christ's perseverance. -2 Thessalonians 3:5 My purpose is that they may be encouraged in heart and united in love, so that they may have the full riches of complete understanding, in order that they may know the mystery of God, namely, Christ. -Colossians 2:2

If you have any encouragement from being united with Christ, if any comfort from his love, if any fellowship with the spirit if any tenderness and compassion, then make my joy complete by being like-minded, having the same love being one in spirit and purpose. -Philippians 2:1-2

And in every sort of evil that deceives those who are perishing. They perish because they refused to love the truth and so be saved. -2 Thessalonians 2:10 For the love of money is a root of all kinds of evil. Some people, eager for money, have wandered from the faith and pierced themselves with many griefs. -1 Timothy 6:10 But you man of God, flee from all this and pursue righteousness, godliness, faith, love, endurance and gentleness. -1 Timothy 6:11

Teach the older men to be temperate, worthy of respect, self-controlled, and sound in faith, in love and in endurance. -Titus 2:2 What you heard from me, keep as the pattern of sound teaching, faith and love in Christ Jesus. -2 Timothy 1:13 For God did not give us a spirit of fear, but a spirit of power, of love and of self-discipline. -2 Timothy 1:7 At one time we too were foolish, disobedient, deceived and enslaved by all kinds of passions and pleasures. We lived in malice and envy, being hated and hating one another. But when the kindness and love of God our savior appeared, he saved us through the washing of rebirth and renewal by the Holy Spirit. -Titus 3:3-5

Keep your lives from the love of money and be content with what you have, because God has said, "Never will I leave you; never will I forsake you." -Hebrews 13:5 God is not unjust; he will not forget your work and the love you have shown him as you helped his people and you continue to help them. -Hebrews 6:10 Your love has given me great joy and encouragement, because you, brother, have refreshed the hearts of the saints. -Philemon 1:7 And let us consider how we may spur one another on toward love and good deeds. -Hebrews 10:24 Keep on loving each other as brothers. -Hebrews 13:1

Show proper respect to everyone, love the brotherhood of believers, fear God, honor the king. -1 Peter 2:17 For "Whoever would love life and see good days must keep his tongue from evil and his lips from deceitful speech." -1 Peter 3:10 Do not love the world or anything in the world. If anyone loves the world, the love of the father is not in him. For everything in the world, the cravings of sinful man, the lust of his eyes and the boasting of what he has and does comes not from the father, but from the world. The world and its desires pass away but the man who does the will of God lives forever. -1 John 2:15-17

But if anyone obeys his word, God's love is truly made complete in him. This is how we know we are in him: whoever claims to live in him must walk as Jesus did. -1 John 2:5-6 And this is love: that we walk in obedience to his commands. As you have heard from the beginning, his command is that you walk in love. -2 John 1:6 Those whom I love I rebuke and discipline. So be earnest and repent. -Revelation 3:19

Keep yourselves in God's love as you wait for the mercy of our Lord Jesus Christ to bring you to eternal life. -Jude 1:21 Though you have not seen him, you love him; and even though you do not see him now, you believe in him and are filled with an inexpressible and glorious joy. -1 Peter 1:8 Listen my dear brothers: has not God chosen those who are poor in the eyes of the world to be rich in faith and to inherit the kingdom he promised to those who love him? -James 2:5

If anyone has material possessions and sees a brother or sister in need but has no pity on them, how can the love of God be in that person? Dear children, let us not love with words or speech but with actions and in truth. -1 John 3:17-18 How great is the love the father has lavished on us, that we should be called children of God! -1 John 3:1 Everyone who believes that Jesus is the Christ is born of God, and everyone who loves the father loves his child as well. This is how we know that we love the children of God: by loving God and carrying out his commands. In fact, this is love for God: to keep his commands. And his commands are not burdensome. -1 John 5:1-3 Now that you have purified yourselves by obeying the truth so that you have sincere love for your brothers, love one another deeply from the heart. -1 Peter 1:22

Blessed is the man who perseveres under trial, because when he has stood the test, he will receive the crown of life that God has promised to those who love him. -James 1:12 If I speak in the tongues of men or of angels, but do not have love, I am only a resounding gong or a clanging cymbal. If I have the gift of prophecy and can fathom all mysteries and all knowledge, and if I have a faith that can move mountains, but do not have love, I am nothing. If I give all I possess to the poor and give over my body to hardship that I may boast, but do not have love, I gain nothing. Love is patient, love is kind. It does not envy, it does not boast, it is not proud. It does not dishonor others, it is not self-seeking, it is not easily angered, it keeps no record of wrongs. Love does not delight in evil but rejoices with the truth. It always protects, always trusts, always hopes, always perseveres. Love never fails. But where there are prophecies, they will cease; where there are tongues, they will be stilled; where there is knowledge, it will pass away. For we know in part and we prophesy in part, but when completeness comes, what is in part disappears. When I was a child, I talked like a child, I thought like a child, I reasoned like a child. When I became a man, I put the ways of childhood behind me. For now we see only a reflection as in a mirror; then we shall see face to face. Now I know in part; then I shall know fully, even as I am fully known. And now these three remain: faith, hope and love. But the greatest of these is love. -1 Corinthians 13

But the fruit of the spirit is love, joy, peace, patience, kindness, goodness, faithfulness, gentleness and self-control. -Galatians 5:22-23

Finally, all of you, live in harmony with one another; be sympathetic, love as brothers, be compassionate and humble. -1 Peter 3:8 Finally brothers, good bye. Aim for perfection, listen to my appeal, be of one mind, live in peace. And the God of love and peace will be with you. -2 Corinthians 13:11

Questions for Reflection and Discussion

1. In the bible we know that God demonstrates His love for mankind by sacrificing His only Son. How can we show love in the form of hope to a world that doesn't know Jesus?

2. Name a time in your life that you demonstrated a selfless act of love.

3. How did you feel after your selfless deed was done?

4. What are some ways as a church that you can show Non-Christians your love for them?

CHAPTER 8

ENCOURAGEMENT

Encouragement: Here are the ABC's of encouragement.

A. Encouragement is an act of love that brings hope, comfort and relief to those who are suffering.

B. Continuous encouragement empowers a person to persevere. Especially when they are in a time of trial, or a time of training and transition.

C. There may be a vast difference between encouragement and instruction!

D. Many people make the mistake of instructing and rebuking, thinking that they are encouraging someone by telling them what needs to be done in order to fix their situation or by making judgment calls regarding their decisions.

E. Be very careful what you choose to say to someone who has been led into a storm. Because your words have the power to build up or destroy that person's spirit.

F. Remember, God is the one who leads a person into a time of training and transition. Anyone who asks to be used by God and is willing to bear fruit for the kingdom of God will be pruned; so that he will bear even more fruit.

G. Don't make the mistake of interfering with God's plan by trying to fix a person's situation. When you try to fix a person's situation you become an instructor and not an encourager!

H. God will always give instructions to the person who is going through a storm. He is the one who leads and instructs a person through their training and transition period, not you.

I. If it is necessary, God will use others, those of His own choosing; to give a word of encouragement for those in need of instruction or direction. If you think God has given you a word of encouragement, make sure it is of God and not yourself or the devil.

J. God has a perfect plan for His child's deliverance. He will let them know what needs to be done in order for them to persevere and get their victory!

K. When God puts a person through a pruning process, they will go through tremendous suffering. It is only through suffering that God is able to train and teach a person the things they need to know in order to have a victorious ministry. It is through suffering that you attain the knowledge and wisdom of God!

L. When a person goes through a tremendous loss. They experience tremendous shock to their mind and emotions. They immediately question God's reasoning for their loss. They feel as if God has abandoned them or as if God is punishing them for some unknown reason.

M. Allow that person to grieve and talk about their situation. It is only human for a person to go through feelings of helplessness and hopelessness, especially when their loss is great. Don't misconstrue their grief, frustration, or anger over their situation as negativism or lack of faith.

N. Don't be harsh or use reckless words when you're speaking to someone who is enduring a pruning process, because your words will remain in their mind and heart for the duration of their trial. Satan will use your words to bring them down. So be careful to use words that promote healing and relief.

O. Remember this: God expects us to encourage one another daily! This is our obligation to one another as members of Christ's body. It is not your right to judge or make an assumption as to why a person is going through a trial or a time of testing! So don't be quick to instruct or rebuke a person because of their situation, but be imitators of Christ and show love compassion and support in their time of need!

P. When Job went through his time of testing, he longed for encouragement and comfort, but instead he received rebuking, instruction, ridicule and scorn. Job was hurt because he knew he had been totally obedient to God. He knew he had developed a right relationship with God. Yet people treated him as if he had done something wrong when all he ever did was everything right.

Q. Don't make the mistake of treating someone the way Job's friends, family members and acquaintances treated him. Or you may find yourself in the same situation as Job's friends. God vindicated Job and He rebuked his friends for what they had said.

R. It takes great love, compassion, commitment and patience in order to be an effective encourager! If you lack these qualities you will always be an overbearing instructor.

S. When you encourage, comfort, and show compassion, you become a powerful tool that God can use to help a person persevere. If you instruct and rebuke you become a powerful tool that the devil can use to interfere with God's plan.

T. The devil will plant his words of instruction and rebuking in your mind so that his words will be used to miss direct a person's thoughts. His goal is to gain control over a person's situation, in that, he can get them to ignore God's instructions and follow his instructions down a path that can only bring confusion, frustration and bitter disappointment. If he can accomplish this, he has the opportunity to destroy that person's faith in God and possibly steal their victory. His ultimate goal is to destroy the work God is doing in them, by distracting them to do something else.

U. If you desire to be used by the Lord there will be a time in your life when God will lead you into a period of training and transition for some form of ministry. The one consistent thing that you can count on is that you will wait on the Lord. The waiting process is very painful and frustrating, both mentally and emotionally, because the process may go on for years. The frustration comes from not knowing why you have been led into this process, or where God is leading you, or how long it's going to take before God has completed His work in you.

V. When the devil sees that you are waiting on the Lord, he will use this time as an opportunity to attack your faith in God. Notice how I said he will use this time, because the more God wants to use you, my friend, the more the waves of attack will be for you. It is not pleasant to think about, but it is the reality of what a relationship with God is all about. Just remember that means the greater the victory you will have from the Lord. It is during a waiting process that a person needs encouragement the MOST! The devil will always use people to bring you down when you are waiting on the Lord. People who instruct and rebuke become your worst friends. The devil will use them as a voice box.

W. People who instruct and rebuke are also people who have a tendency to make judgments regarding your situation. If you have been in a trial for a while, maybe even years; people will start to doubt your faith in God, your obedience to God, and your ability to hear from God. They will make assumptions or state accusations as to why you are still in your situation. Don't let Satan use these people to beat you down with their accusations. Ignore their statements and avoid making contact with them.

X. Remember, God does not lead obedient children into a refining process to discipline or punish them. It is only because a child has been obedient, and is willing to bear fruit for the kingdom of God. God leads them into a process of training and transition for the sake of His ministry. So don't be quick to judge a person because of their situation, but be quick to show Christian love, compassion and encouragement. You will never understand what a person is going through unless you have experienced their situation for yourself. If you have an income, a spouse, a family, a home, your health and a structured life, you cannot possibly imagine what it is like to lose everything! The person who has lost everything knows that you can't understand, because you don't! Don't have that attitude that you have to "pull someone up by their bootstraps" and move them on when that person has nothing left to help them move forward. Also, they can't move forward if God has them in a holding position! God is the only one who will deliver and move someone forward, and He will do it in His way and in His due time!

Y. If you find yourself in the middle of a storm and you have been totally obedient; by making every effort to live for God and please Him in all your ways, don't beat yourself up over your situation and don't let others bring you down. God may be re-arranging your life through a tremendous loss or suffering, but it is only temporarily. God understands that your faith can get severely beaten down. He knows your hurt and pain, He counts your tears. God also knows what He has in store for you at the end of your storm. God loves you. He will encourage you; He will also bring someone in your life to help encourage you along the way. He knows your needs, He also know the value of encouragement; after all I am sure He had to encourage his Son down that long road of suffering to get Him to the cross and to endure the sins of humankind on the cross!

Z. When God leads a person into a storm He has them there for a reason. Don't get in the way of God's plan by trying to fix a person's situation. When a person is waiting on the Lord this process can go on for years. Every year that goes by just brings more hardship and disappointment. The longer a trial lasts the more broken a person becomes. That person's feelings of doubt, hurt, anger, frustration and confusion only intensifies as time goes by.

Encouragement comes in many different forms!

1. Being a good listener makes a person feel loved and valued!

2. A good listener shows compassion and empathy regarding a person's feelings!

3. A good listener allows a person to vent their frustrations, doubts, hurt and anguish without making judgments or accusations regarding their situation.

4. Pray daily for a person that is enduring a trial. Let them know that they are in your daily prayers. Make sure you spend time with them in prayer because it will lift their spirit.

5. Show a person that you care about them and are there for them in their time of need by sending them a card, letter or flowers.

6. Sending monetary gifts will bring relief and joy to those who have endured tremendous loss. Any kind of love gift, whether it is food, clothing or aid for utilities will lift a person's burden and encourage them to keep on persevering.

7. Remember those who are going through a storm during the holiday seasons. The holiday seasons are the toughest to get through.

8. A kind word or even the smallest of gestures goes a very long way. You'll never know how much a person values your encouragement until you experience a storm yourself.

9. Showing love through your deeds is the greatest form of encouragement you can give a brother or sister in Christ. Encouraging others is a necessary function of our daily walk with Christ.

Wisdom from God's Heart

Then the church throughout Judea, Galilee and Samaria enjoyed a time of peace and was strengthened. Living in the fear of the Lord and encouraged by the Holy Spirit, it increased in numbers. -Acts 9:31 When Apollos wanted to go to Achaia, the brothers and sisters encouraged him and wrote to the disciples there to welcome him. When he arrived, he was a great help to those who by grace had believed. -Acts 18:27 After Paul and Silas came out of the prison, they went to Lydia's house, where they met with the brothers and sisters and encouraged them. Then they left. -Acts 16:40

Judas and Silas, who themselves were prophets, said much to encourage and strengthen the believers. -Acts 15:32 When Barnabas arrived and saw what the grace of God had done, he was glad and encouraged them all to remain true to the Lord with all their hearts. -Acts 11:23   Paul traveled through Macedonia, speaking many words of encouragement to the people, and finally arrived in Greece. -Acts 20:2   For everything that was written in the past was written to teach us, so that through the endurance taught in the Scriptures and the encouragement they provide we might have hope. May the God who gives endurance and encouragement give you the same attitude of mind toward each other that Christ Jesus had. -Romans 15:4-5

For you can all prophesy in turn so that everyone may be instructed and encouraged. -1 Corinthians 14:31   Remember this: Whoever sows sparingly will also reap sparingly, and whoever sows generously will also reap generously. -2 Corinthians 9:6 Therefore if you have any encouragement from being united with Christ, if any comfort from his love, if any common sharing in the Spirit, if any tenderness and compassion, then make my joy complete by being like-minded, having the same love, being one in spirit and of one mind. - Philippians 2:1-2   I have spoken to you with great frankness; I take great pride in you. I am greatly encouraged; in all our troubles my joy knows no bounds. -2 Corinthians 7:4   My goal is that they may be encouraged in heart and united in love, so that they may have the full riches of complete understanding, in order that they may know the mystery of God, namely, Christ. -Colossians 2:2

We sent Timothy, who is our brother and co-worker in God's service in spreading the gospel of Christ, to strengthen and encourage you in your faith. -1 Thessalonians 3:2   Therefore, brothers and sisters, in all our distress and persecution we were encouraged about you because of your faith. -1 Thessalonians 3:7   Therefore encourage one another with these words. -1 Thessalonians 4:18

And we urge you, brothers and sisters, warn those who are idle and disruptive, encourage the disheartened, help the weak, be patient with everyone. -1 Thessalonians 5:14   Therefore encourage one another and build each other up, just as in fact you are doing. -1 Thessalonians 5:11   Preach the word; be prepared in season and out of season; correct, rebuke and encourage with great patience and careful instruction. -2 Timothy 4:2 These, then, are the things you should teach. Encourage and rebuke with all authority. Do not let anyone despise you. -Titus 2:15

Make every effort to live in peace with everyone and to be holy; without holiness no one will see the Lord. -Hebrews 12:14 But encourage one another daily, as long as it is called "Today," so that none of you may be hardened by sin's deceitfulness. -Hebrews 3:13 God did this so that, by two unchangeable things in which it is impossible for God to lie, we who have fled to take hold of the hope set before us may be greatly encouraged. -Hebrews 6:18

Finally, brothers and sisters, rejoice! Strive for full restoration, encourage one another, be of one mind, live in peace. And the God of love and peace will be with you. -2 Corinthians 13:11 If it is to encourage, then give encouragement; if it is giving, then give generously; if it is to lead, do it diligently; if it is to show mercy, do it cheerfully. -Romans 12:8 May our Lord Jesus Christ himself and God our Father, who loved us and by his grace gave us eternal encouragement and good hope. -2 Thessalonians 2:16

Questions for Reflection and Discussion

1. List all the people that you know of right now that are struggling in their life in some way.

2. Think of one way that you could make an impact on the lives of each person that you know is struggling in life.

3. In what way could your church help these people out?

4. Pick one person from your list. Find something that you may be able to do to help that person out.

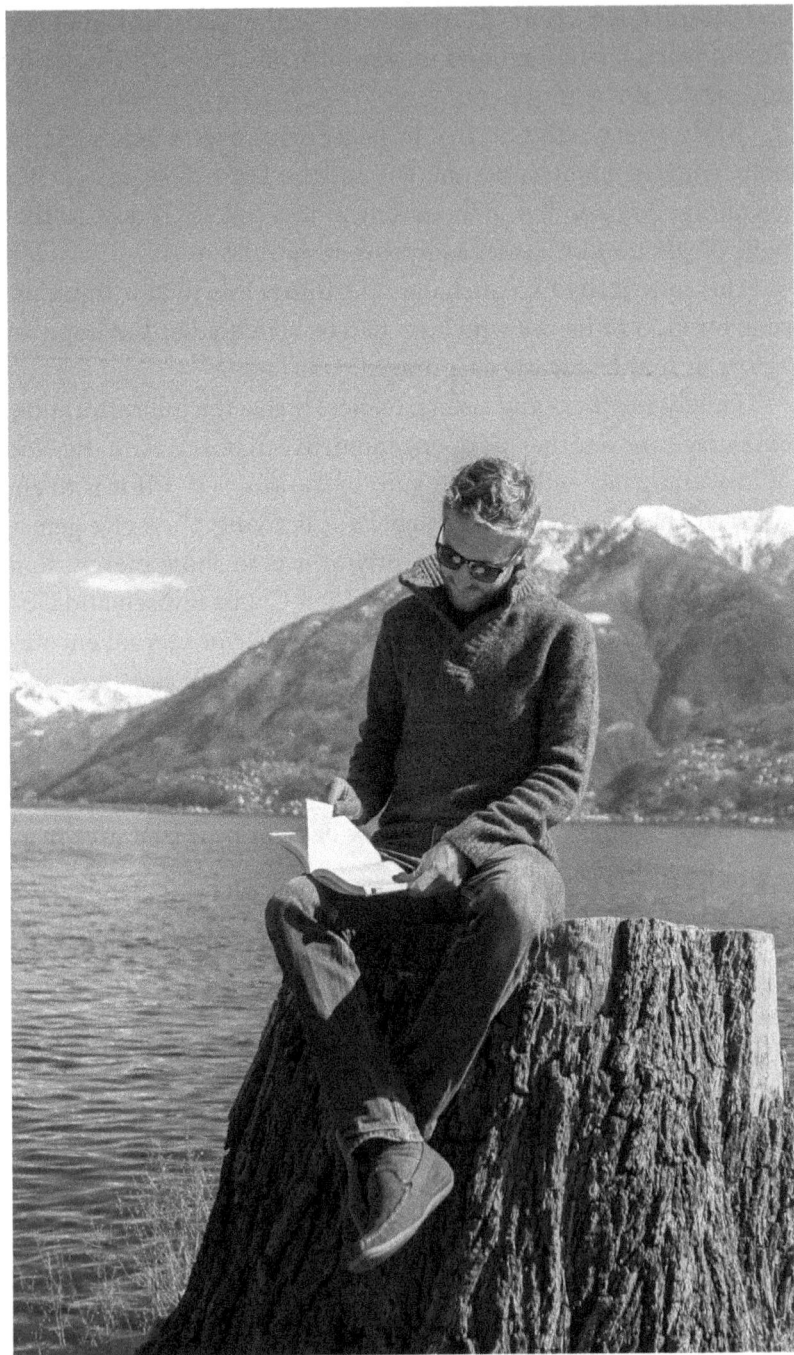

CHAPTER NINE

JESUS' TEACHINGS

In your life there comes a time when you realize that you can't live on your own anymore, you're tired of feeling empty inside and no matter what you try to do you need to have more to achieve satisfaction. No matter what you do or how many things you strive for and try to attain to make you happy, you still feel that emptiness, that void, like somethings missing. No matter how many great friends or people you surround yourself with, you feel that no one understands you as a person. You need peace, you need comfort, and you want to have security, knowing that everything will be all right. In that moment, it feel like all these things are eating you up inside and are weighing heavy on your heart and you just feel like you want to die and scream out at the top of your lungs. It is then that you realize the only way to become complete is to have Jesus take hold of your life. So you decide to become a Christian.

For me, I remember where I was at when I had decided to become a Christian. I was a teenager, and at that point in my life I had so many things going in the wrong direction. The biggest concern for me was that I felt all alone. I never really had a father who was there for me, in the ways that I had needed, and I felt so out of place when it came to my own family. I felt like I was the outcast of my family and that I didn't really belong or fit in. I was having trouble in school, always getting bullied. I didn't really have any friends or really know how to be a friend. I got so tired of being alone and having no one there to believe in me and be there for me. So I ended up turning to God for help. I told Him that I would dedicate my life to Him if he would be my Father and if He would be there for me and take care of me and show me the love that I was looking for in my life.

So you make that decision. Maybe it was at a church function or with a friend. Maybe it was a very emotional time in your life, like mine was, or maybe it was just as simple as this is the right thing to do. So you do it, you ask Jesus into your heart, you confess He is Lord, and you ask Him to take away your sins. You ask Him to guide you and become Lord of your life. There, you have surrendered. You gave Him control of your life.

You feel great, you feel free; it feels like you have this huge weight lifted off your shoulder, and you feel ten feet taller. You say to yourself, "I did it!" You just made a life changing commitment and it feels good. So, after that awesome moment when the feeling good is starting to fade, you think to yourself, "OK now what?" Now you're wondering, "I made this commitment, so what do I do from here, where do I go, how do I live, how do I keep on this path?"

These verses from Scripture will give you understanding about what you need to do, and how you need to act in life as a Christian. They will help back up the tremendous life changing decision that you just made. You're now on your way to being victorious. Remember the only way to be victorious in your life is by seeking after the WAY, the TRUTH and the LIFE!

Wisdom from God's Heart

"If anyone would come after me, he must deny himself and take up his cross and follow me. For whoever wants to save his life will lose it, but whoever loses his life for me will find it. What good will it be for a man if he gains the whole world, yet forfeits his soul? Or what can a man give in exchange for his soul? For the son of man is going to come in his Father's glory with his angels, and then he will reward each person according to what he has done." -Matthew 16:24-27 "Whoever serves me must follow me; and where I am, my servant also will be. My Father will honor the one who serves me." -John 12:26 "I tell you the truth, no one who has left home or brothers or sisters or mother or father or children or fields for me and the gospel will fail to receive a hundred times as much in this present age and in the age to come, eternal life." -Mark 10:29-30

"If you hold to my teaching, you are really my disciples. Then you will know the truth, and the truth will set you free!" -John 8:31-32 "Whoever has my commands and obeys them, he is the one who loves me. He who loves me will be loved by my Father, and I too will love him and show myself to him. If anyone loves me, he will obey my teaching. My father will love him and we will make our home with him. He who does not love me will not obey my teaching. These words you hear are not my own; they belong to the Father who sent me." -John 14:21, 23-24 "For I have come down from heaven not to do my will but to do the will of him who sent me. And this is the will of him who sent me, that I shall lose none of all that he has given me, but raise them up at the last day. For my Father's will is that everyone who looks to the son and believes in him shall have eternal life, and I will raise him up at the last day." -John 6:38-40

"I have come that they may have life, and have it more abundantly." -John 10:10 "For the son of man did not come to be served, but to serve; and to give his life as a ransom for many." -Matthew 20:28 "I am the light of the world. Whoever follows me will never walk in darkness, but will have the light of life." -John 8:12 "Everyone who does evil hates the light, and will not come into the light for fear that his deeds will be exposed. But whoever lives by the truth comes into the light, so that it may be seen plainly that what he has done has been done through God." -John 3:20-21

"I am the good shepherd; I know my sheep and my sheep know me. My sheep listen to my voice; I know them and they follow me. Just as the Father knows me and I know the Father, and I lay down my life for the sheep. I give them eternal life, and they shall never perish; no one can snatch them out of my hand. I and the Father are one. I have other sheep that are not of this sheep pen. I must bring them also. They too will listen to my voice, and there shall be one flock and one shepherd. The reason my Father loves me is that I lay down my life, only to take it up again. No one takes it from me, but I lay it down of my own accord. I have authority to lay it down and authority to take it up again. This command I received from my Father." -John 10:14, 27, 15, 28, 30, 16-18

"My command is this; love each other as I have loved you. Greater love has no one than this, that he lay down his life for his friends. You are my friends if you do what I command." -John 15:12-14 "I am the resurrection and the life. He who believes in me will live, even though he dies; and whoever lives and believes in me will never die." -John 11:25-26

"When a man believes in me, he does not believe in me only, but in the one who sent me. I have come into the world as a light, so that no one who believes in me should stay in darkness. As for the person who hears my words but does not keep them, I do not judge him. For I did not come to judge the world, but to save it. There is a judge for the one who rejects me and does not accept my words; that very word which I spoke will condemn him at the last day. For I did not speak of my own accord, but the Father who sent me commanded me what to say and how to say it. I know that his command leads to eternal life. So whatever I say is just what the Father has told me to say." -John 12:44, 46-50 "I am the way and the truth and the life. No one comes to the Father except through me. If you really knew me, you would know my Father as well." -John 14:6-7

"The words I say to you are not just my own. Rather, it is the Father, living in me, who is doing the work. Believe me when I say that I am in the Father and the Father is in me. -John 14:10-11 "I am the vine; you are the branches. If a man remains in me and I in him, he will bear much fruit; apart from me you can do nothing. If anyone does not remain in me, he is like a branch that is thrown away and withers; such branches are picked up, thrown in to the fire and burned. If you remain in me and my words remain in you, ask whatever you wish, and it will be given to you. This is to my Father's glory, that you bear much fruit, showing yourselves to be my disciples." -John 15:5-8

"Do not work for food that spoils, but for food that endures to eternal life, which the son of man will give you. On him God the Father has placed his seal of approval." -John 6:27 "Watch out! Be on your guard against all kinds of greed; a man's life does not consist in the abundance of his possessions." -Luke 12:15 "Do not store up for yourselves treasures on earth, where moth and rust destroy, and where thieves break in and steal. But store up for yourselves treasure in heaven, where moth and rust do not destroy, and where thieves do not break in and steal. For where your treasure is, there your heart will be also. -Matthew 6:19-21

"No one can serve two masters. Either he will hate the one and love the other, or he will be devoted to the one and despise the other. You cannot serve both God and money." -Matthew 6:24 "Do not worry, saying what shall we eat, or what shall we drink, or what shall we wear, for the pagans run after all these things, and your heavenly Father knows you need them. But seek first his kingdom and his righteousness, and all these things will be given to you as well." -Matthew 6:31-33 "Come to me, all who are weary and burdened, and I will give you rest. Take my yoke upon you and learn from me, for I am gentle and humble in heart, and you will find rest for your souls. For my yoke is easy and my burden is light." -Matthew 11:28-30

"I say to you: ask and it will be given to you; seek and you will find; knock and the door will be opened to you. For everyone who asks receives; he who seeks finds; and to him who knocks, the door will be opened." -Luke 11:9-10 " I tell you the truth, whatever you ask for in prayer, believed that you have received it, and it will be yours. And when you stand praying, if you hold anything against anyone, forgive him, so that your father in heaven may forgive you your sins." -Mark 11:24-25

"For if you forgive men when they sin against you. Your heavenly Father will also forgive you. But if you do not forgive men their sins, your Father in heaven will not forgive your sins." -Matthew 6:14-15 "Lord," asked Peter, "How many times shall I forgive my brother when he sins against me? Up to seven times?" Jesus answered, "I tell you, not seven times, but seventy-seven times." -Matthew 18: 21-22

"I tell you who hear me: love your enemies, do good to those who hate you, bless those who curse you, pray for those who mistreat you. So that you may be sons of your Father in heaven. Be perfect, therefore, as your heavenly Father is perfect. If someone strikes you on the cheek turn to him the other also. If someone takes your cloak do not stop him from taking your tunic. Give to everyone who asks you. And if anyone takes what belongs to you, do not demand it back. Do to others as you would have them do to you." -Luke 6:27-28, Matthew 5:48, Luke 6:29-31 "Do not be afraid, little flock, your Father has been pleased to give you the kingdom. Sell your possessions and give to the poor provide purses for yourselves that will not wear out, a treasure in heaven that will not be exhausted, where no thief comes near and no moth destroys. -Luke 12:32-33

"When you give a luncheon or dinner, do not invite your friends, your brothers or relatives or your rich neighbors; if you do, they may invite you back and so you will be repaid. But when you give a banquet, invite the poor, the crippled, the lame, the blind, and you will be blessed. Although they cannot repay you, you will be repaid at the resurrection of the righteous." -Luke 14:12-14 "I tell you the truth, whatever you did for one of the least of these brothers of mine, you did for me." -Matthew 25:40 "I tell you the truth, no servant is greater than his master, nor is a messenger greater than the one who sent him. Now that you know these things, you will be blessed if you do them." -John 13:16-17

"Whoever exalts himself will be humbled, and whoever humbles himself will be exalted." - Matthew 23:12 "I tell you the truth, unless you change and become like little children, you will never enter the kingdom of heaven. Whoever humbles himself like a child is the greatest in the kingdom of heaven. And whoever welcomes a child in my name welcomes me. But if anyone causes one of these little ones who believe in me to sin, it would be better for him to have a millstone hung around his neck and to be drowned in the depths of the sea. Woe to the world because of the things that cause people to sin! Such things must come, but woe to the man through whom they come! If your hand causes you to sin, cut it off. It is better for you to enter life maimed than with two hands to go into hell, where the fire never goes out. And if your foot causes you to sin, cut it off. It is better for you to enter life crippled than to have two feel and be thrown into hell. And if your eye causes you to sin, pluck it out. It is better for you to enter the kingdom of God with one eye than to have two eyes and be thrown into hell, where their worm does not die, and the fire is not quenched!" -Matthew 18:3-7, Mark 9:43-48 "Do not be afraid of those who kill the body but cannot kill the soul. Rather, be afraid of the one who can destroy both soul and body in hell." - Matthew 10:28

"You have heard that it was said, "Do not commit adultery." But I tell you that anyone who looks at a woman lustfully has already committed adultery with her in his heart." -Matthew 5:27-28 "It has been said, " Anyone who divorces his wife must give her a certificate of divorce," but I tell you that anyone who divorces his wife, except for marital unfaithfulness, causes her to become an adulteress, and anyone who marries the divorced woman commits adultery." -Matthew 5:31-32

"Again, you have heard that it was said to the people long ago, "do not break your oath, but keep the oaths you have made to the Lord." But I tell you do not swear at all: either by heaven, for it is God's throne; or by the earth, for it is his footstool; simply let your "yes" be "yes," and your "no", "no." anything beyond this comes from the evil one." -Matthew 5:33-35, 37

"Do not murder, anyone who murders will be subject to judgment. But I tell you that anyone who is angry with his brother will be subject to judgment. And anyone who says, "you fool!" will be in danger of the fire of hell." -Matthew 5:21-22 "Do not judge, or you too will be judged, for in the same way you judge others, you will be judged, and with the measure you use, it will be measured to you." -Matthew 7:1-2

"The good man brings good things out of the good stored up in his heart, and the evil man brings evil things out of the evil stored up in his heart. For out of the overflow of his heart his mouth speaks. I tell you that men will have to give an account on the Day of Judgment for every careless word they have spoken. For by your words you will be acquitted, and by your words you will be condemned." -Luke 6:45, Matthew 12:36-37

"Anyone who breaks one of the least of these commandments and teaches others to do the same will be called least in the kingdom of heaven, but whoever practices and teaches these commands will be called great in the kingdom of heaven." -Matthew 5:19 "I tell you the truth, everyone who sins is a slave to sin, now a slave has no permanent place in the family, but a son belongs to it forever. So if the son sets you free, you will be free indeed." -John 8:34-36

"Do repent of your sins, for the kingdom of heaven is near." -Matthew 4:17 "I tell you there will be more rejoicing n heaven over one sinner who repents than over ninety-nine righteous persons who do not need to repent." -Luke 15:7 "Every sin and blasphemy will be forgiven men, but the blasphemy against the Holy Spirit will not be forgiven. Anyone who speaks against the son of man will be forgiven, but anyone who speaks against the Holy Spirit will not be forgiven, neither in this age or in the age to come." -Matthew 12:31-32

"I tell you the truth, no one can see the kingdom of God unless he is born again. Unless; he is born of water and spirit, flesh gives birth to flesh, but spirit gives birth to spirit." -John 3:3, 5-6 "The spirit gives life; The flesh counts for nothing. The words I have spoken to you are spirit and they are life." -John 6:63 "I tell you the truth, whoever hears my word and believes him who sent me has eternal life and will not be condemned; he has crossed over from death to life." -John 5:24 "If anyone keeps my word, he will never see death." -John 8:51

"Therefore, everyone who hears these words of mine and puts them into practice is like a wise man who built his house on the rock. The rain came down, the streams rose, and the winds blew and beat against that house; yet it did not fall, because it had its foundation on the rock. But everyone who hears these words of mine and does not put them into practice is a like a foolish man who built his house on the sand. The rain came down, the streams rose, and the winds blew and beat against that house, and it fell with a great crash!" -Matthew 7:24-27 "Who then is the faithful and wise servant, whom the master has put in charge of the servants in his household to give them their food at the proper time? It would be good for that servant whose master finds him doing so when he returns. I tell you the truth, he will put him in charge of all his possessions." - Matthew 24:45-47

"Blessed are those who have not seen, and yet they believe in me!" -John 20:29 "Whoever believes and is baptized will be saved, but whoever does not believe will be condemned." -Mark 16:16 "I am the living one; I was dead, and behold I am alive forever and ever! And I hold the keys to death and Hades." -Revelation 1:18

Questions for Reflection and Discussion

1. How do you feel that we can apply Jesus' teachings in our lives today?

2. Which of Jesus' teachings do you feel is the hardest for you to follow and why?

3. What are some ways that you can be sure that you are following Jesus' teachings correctly?

4. Which of Jesus' teachings is your favorite and why?

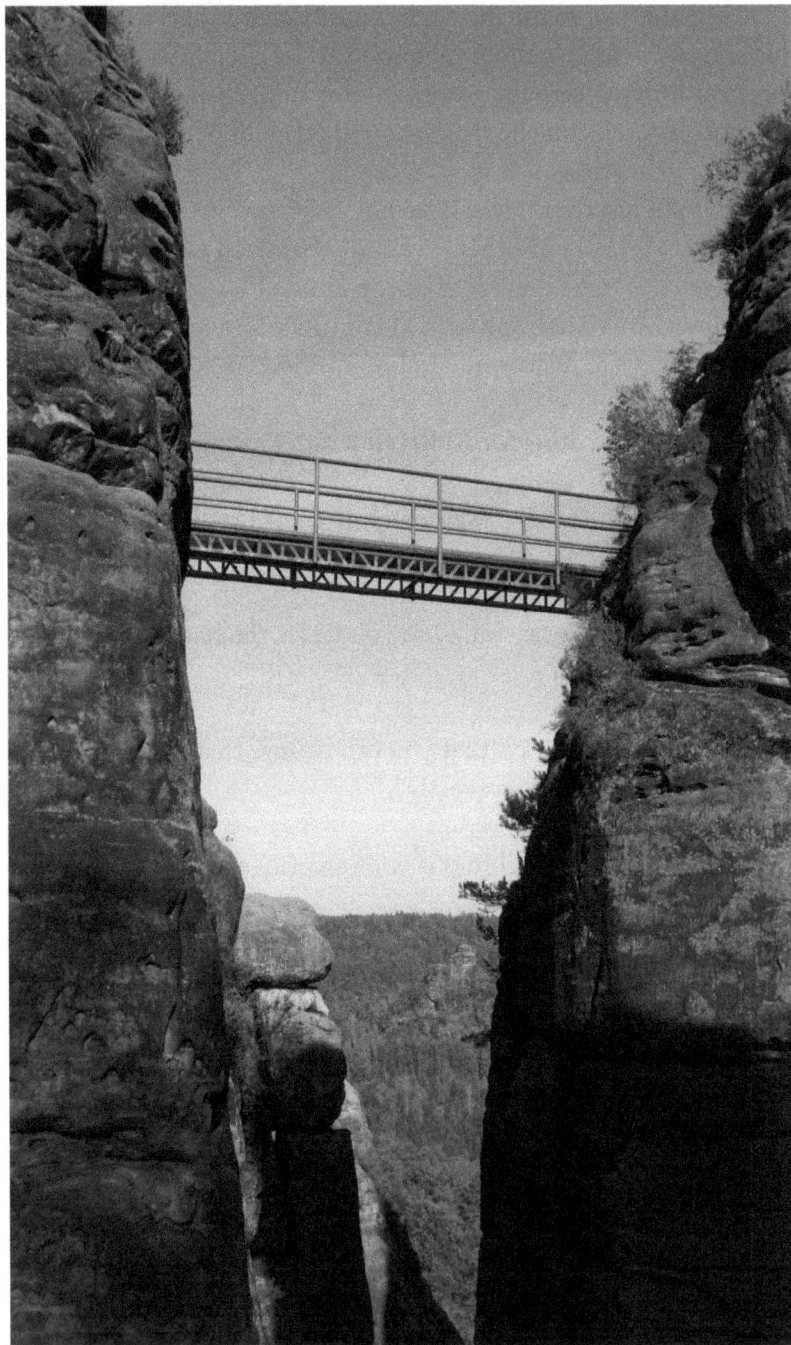

CHAPTER TEN

AUTHORITY

When we think of living a victorious life in Christ, there is one key element that most Christians think of and that element is Faith. Now faith is a great substance to have. It can be a very powerful one at that, but in order to put your faith into action there is one key essential tool that needs to be used. In order to unlock that faith, you need something else so you may be able to take that raw passion you have for the Lord and fulfill that desire to make a difference in this world. If you can master this tool and learn to use it the right way, then your walk with your Heavenly Father will be solid and strong and nothing will get in the way of it.

You see, God didn't send His Son just to die for our sins. If that was the only purpose then God could have had Jesus die for us as a child or as a baby. There is a reason why Jesus died when He did as the sinless sacrifice. God wanted us to learn from Jesus, and that is why Jesus chose to travel this earth with His disciples and why He taught them everything He did. That is the reason why we have the Bible. The men that Jesus taught, recorded these things so that others may learn from it. The biggest tool that people don't know how to use or how to use correctly is authority.

Now some of you might be saying authority? Since when do we have authority? How do you use authority? Here's the deal, when Jesus came to this earth He was God in the form of man. Now, because He was perfect and He was blameless His whole life, He was acceptable to be the offering to bridge the distance from man and God that was created when Adam and Eve sinned in the Garden of Eden. Therefore, He could eliminate the sin that was counted against us. This separated us from the Lord. What also came with that responsibility was the power to overcome evil and the authority to rule over sin and the devil instead of the other way around.

Now, here's where the greatest part comes in, the reason that Jesus did all the miracles and the miraculous healing that He did wasn't to prove that He was the Son of God. Jesus didn't need to prove anything to us; He knew already that He was the Son of God. It was to show us how to live, to get ready to live a life of freedom from sin.

Once the price was paid for sin, then nothing has the right to rule over us. The devil tries to get us to believe he has the power over us and he has the right to rule over us, but he doesn't. When Jesus died He gave us a gift. That gift was the Holy Spirit, who is also God. The Holy Spirit lives in us. So you now have God living inside of you and that also means that the power of God, which is in the Holy Spirit, is also accessible for you to use.

You see it is that power that you have, the gift of the Holy Spirit, Who was promised from Christ. He is living inside you and can guide and teach you in your everyday life. Now you have something you can use to fight the devil with when he tries to use his tactics to keep you in sin. The biggest misconception that people have is that Jesus did all the work. The deed is done; so there is nothing left that I should have to do. Yes, Christ died for our sins. So the punishment for sin, which is eternal separation from God, is no longer a part of your life. Christ set us free. That work is complete.

However, that doesn't mean that just because Jesus died for our sins that the devil and his ways were eliminated. The devil is still here and he is still at work! We are still at war people! If the devil can make us think that he is not around or that we don't have to fight on a daily basis to still stay pure and clean and have a right relationship with our Heavenly Father, then the devil has succeeded and won. It is this very reason, that people aren't using their authority in Christ Jesus through the Holy Spirit, that the world is still as evil as it is.

Two things to remember: One, you have to use your authority in your daily life to be successful and victorious in your walk with Christ. Second, you still need to use your authority to win souls for the kingdom. Regardless of where you are at in life or where you live; you still need to be spreading the Gospel and be winning souls for the kingdom. Like it or not, that still is a command that Jesus gave for us to do until He comes back.

Wisdom from God's Heart

God placed all things under his feet and appointed him to be head over everything for the church, which is his body, the fullness of him who fills everything in every way. -Ephesians 1:22-23 "The thief comes only to steal and kill and destroy; I have come that they may have life, and have it more abundantly!" -John 10:10 "I have given you authority to trample on snakes and scorpions and to overcome all the power of the enemy; nothing will harm you!" -Luke 10:19

For in Christ all the fullness of the Deity lives in bodily form, and in Christ you have been brought to fullness. He is the head over every power and authority. -Colossians 2:9-10 In the presence of God and of Christ Jesus, who will judge the living and the dead, and in view of his appearing and his kingdom, I give you this charge: Preach the word; be prepared in season and out of season; correct, rebuke and encourage—with great patience and careful instruction. -2 Timothy 4:1-2 "And I will ask the Father, and he will give you another advocate to help you and be with you forever." -John 14:16 "I am the way and the truth and the life. No one comes to the Father except through me." -John 14:6

"You are my friends if you do what I command. I no longer call you servants, because a servant does not know his master's business. Instead, I have called you friends, for everything that I learned from my Father I have made known to you." -John 15:14-15 Follow the way of love and eagerly desire gifts of the Spirit, especially prophecy. For anyone who speaks in a tongue does not speak to people but to God. Indeed, no one understands them; they utter mysteries by the Spirit. But the one who prophesies speaks to people for their strengthening, encouraging and comfort. -1 Corinthians 14:1-3

"I will give you the keys of the kingdom of heaven; whatever you bind on earth will be bound in heaven, and whatever you loose on earth will be loosed in heaven." -Matthew 16:19

"Truly I tell you, if you have faith as small as a mustard seed, you can say to this mountain, 'Move from here to there,' and it will move. Nothing will be impossible for you." -Matthew 17:20 "Again, truly I tell you that if two of you on earth agree about anything they ask for, it will be done for them by my Father in heaven." -Matthew 18:19

Since an overseer manages God's household, he must be blameless not overbearing, not quick-tempered, not given to drunkenness, not violent, not pursuing dishonest gain. Rather, he must be hospitable, one who loves what is good, who is self-controlled, upright, holy and disciplined. He must hold firmly to the trustworthy message as it has been taught, so that he can encourage others by sound doctrine and refute those who oppose it. -Titus 1:7-9 "From the days of John the Baptist until now the kingdom of heaven suffers violence, and the violent take it by force." -Matthew 11:12

"I am the vine; you are the branches. If you remain in me and I in you, you will bear much fruit; apart from me you can do nothing. If you do not remain in me, you are like a branch that is thrown away and withers; such branches are picked up, thrown into the fire and burned. If you remain in me and my words remain in you, ask whatever you wish, and it will be done for you. This is to my Father's glory, that you bear much fruit, showing yourselves to be my disciples." -John 15:5-8

"You did not choose me, but I chose you and appointed you so that you might go and bear fruit, fruit that will last and so that whatever you ask in my name the Father will give you." -John 15:16 "I tell you the truth, whoever believes in me will do the works I have been doing, and they will do even greater things than these, because I am going to the Father. And I will do whatever you ask in my name, so that the Father may be glorified in the Son. You may ask me for anything in my name, and I will do it. -John 14:12-14

"Teacher," said John, "We saw a man driving out demons in your name and we told him to stop, because he was not one of us." "Do not stop him," Jesus said. "No one who does a miracle in my name can in the next moment say anything bad about me, for whoever is not against us is for us. I tell you the truth, anyone who gives you a cup of water in my name because you belong to Christ will certainly not lose his reward." -Mark 9:38-41 Early in the morning, as Jesus was on his way back to the city, he was hungry. Seeing a fig tree by the road, he went up to it but found nothing on it except leaves. Then he said to it, "May you never bear fruit again!" Immediately the tree withered. When the disciples saw this, they were amazed. "How did the fig tree wither so quickly?" they asked. Jesus replied, "I tell you the truth, if you have faith and do not doubt, not only can you do what was done to the fig tree, but also you can say to this mountain, 'Go, throw yourself into the sea,' and it will be done. If you believe, you will receive whatever you ask for in prayer." -Matthew 21:18-22

If anyone speaks, they should do so as one who speaks the very words of God. If anyone serves, they should do so with the strength God provides, so that in all things God may be praised through Jesus Christ. To him be the glory and the power for ever and ever. Amen. -1 Peter 4:11 Gracious words are a honeycomb, sweet to the soul and healing to the bones. -Proverbs 16:24 The soothing tongue is a tree of life, but a perverse tongue crushes the spirit. -Proverbs 15:4 A cheerful heart is good medicine, but a crushed spirit dries up the bones. -Proverbs 17:22 The lips of the righteous nourish many, but fools die for lack of sense. -Proverbs 10:21 The fruit of the righteous is a tree of life, and the one who is wise saves lives. -Proverbs 11:30

In the way of righteousness there is life; along that path is immortality. -Proverbs 12:28 Since, then, you have been raised with Christ, set your hearts on things above, where Christ is, seated at the right hand of God. -Colossians 3:1 Out of his fullness we have all received grace in place of grace already given. -John 1:16

For the kingdom of God is not a matter of talk but of power.

-1 Corinthians 4:20 "If you hold to my teaching, you are really my disciples." -John 8:31 "This is to my Father's glory, that you bear much fruit, showing yourselves to be my disciples." -John 15:8 "All authority in heaven and on earth has been given to me. Therefore go and make disciples of all nations, baptizing them in the name of the Father and of the Son and of the Holy Spirit, and teaching them to obey everything I have commanded you. And surely I am with you always, to the very end of the age." -Matthew 28:18-20

"Whoever believes and is baptized will be saved, but whoever does not believe will be condemned. And these signs will accompany those who believe: In my name they will drive out demons; they will speak in new tongues; they will pick up snakes with their hands; and when they drink deadly poison, it will not hurt them at all; they will place their hands on sick people, and they will get well." -Mark 16:16-18 Never be lacking in zeal, but keep your spiritual fervor, serving the Lord. -Romans 12:11 "I tell you the truth, whoever obeys my word will never see death." -John 8:51

Questions for Reflection and Discussion

1. How do you use your authority in your everyday life?

2. What are some ways that you can become stronger in your knowledge of the Word of God?

3. If the Bible is the only weapon we have against the devil and his schemes, how important is it that we know the Bible?

4. How much time do you spend in the Word of God? Do you memorize scripture verses? Do you think it is important to have scripture memorized? If so, why?

5. What are some ways that you can keep each other accountable in knowing the Word of God better?

CHAPTER ELEVEN

HEAVEN

Heaven, it is the final destination as many people like to call it. So what is it about Heaven that makes it so special? Heaven is a perfect place where you can live for eternity with your Heavenly Father and your Lord Jesus Christ. Nobody really knows what Heaven is like in all of it's glory. The Apostle John was given a glimpse of Heaven when he wrote the Revelation. I think everyone has their own idea of how Heaven will play out for them. From reading the Bible, I know that in Heaven there is no more pain and suffering, you will have joy, peace and happiness like you never had before. There will be no need for the Sun in Heaven for God will light up Heaven with His radiance, leaving no place for even a shadow. I know that Jesus has been in Heaven a long time preparing a place for us, and one day He will come back and take us home to be with Him for eternity. Scripture clearly states that getting to Heaven isn't just as easy as walking through the automatic doors at Walmart.

The biggest misconception about Heaven today, is this, "We get to Heaven based on how good we are here on earth." In a sense, we do get to Heaven based on good works, but not by our good works! We get to Heaven based on the completed works of Jesus Christ. Here is my best analogy to explain how Heaven works. Salvation is like a ticket to Heaven. Heaven is the concert, now just because you have a ticket to the concert doesn't mean you are going. You still have to have a personal relationship with Jesus and allow Him to drive you to the concert, and help you find your seat once you get to the arena. The same is true of Heaven. Salvation is a free gift, but you still have to work out your Salvation by obedience to the Father, and living a righteous life, laying down your life for Christ. There are some people who think that since they are saved by Christ's finished work on the cross, they can just go on sinning and God will forgive them. While we are saved by God's grace through faith in Christ, good works will result from a true saving faith. So, your good works are evidence of your saving faith. This is very different from saying that we are saved by being a good person. While the Bible teaches that we are saved by God's grace through faith, the Bible does not teach "easy believism." True Christians will repent of their sins continually and surrender their life to God on a daily basis. Heaven is going to be the most amazing experience that any of us could possibly imagine. The path that leads us to our heavenly home isn't the easiest, but it is definitely worth it.

Wisdom from God's Heart

"Let him who has ears to hear let him hear." -Luke 14:35 "Whoever acknowledges me before men, I will also acknowledge him before my father in heaven. But whoever disowns me before men, I will disown him before my father in heaven." -Matthew 10:32-33 "I tell you the truth if anyone keeps my word he will never see death." -John 8:51 "Be dressed and ready for service and keep your lamps burning, like men waiting for their master to return from a wedding banquet, so that when he comes and knocks they can immediately open the door for him. It will be good for those servants whose master finds them watching when he comes. I tell you the truth, he will dress himself to serve, will have them recline at the table and will come and wait on them. -Luke 12:35-37

Do you not know that the wicked will not inherit the kingdom of God? Do not be deceived: neither the sexually immoral, nor idolaters, nor adulterers, nor males prostitutes, nor homosexual offenders, nor drunkards, nor slanderers, nor swindlers will inherit the kingdom of God. -1 Corinthians 6:9-10 Do not be deceived: God cannot be mocked. A man reaps what he sows. The one who sows to please his sinful nature, from that nature he will reap destruction; the one who sows to please the spirit, from the spirit will reap eternal life. -Galatians 6:6-10 The acts of sinful nature are obvious; Sexual immorality, impurity and debauchery; idolatry, witchcraft, hatred, discord, jealousy, fits of rage, selfish ambition, dissensions, factions, and envy, drunkenness, orgies, and the like. I warn you, as I did before, those that live like this will not enter the kingdom of heaven. -Galatians 5:19-21

"Not everyone who says to me, "Lord, Lord" will enter the kingdom of heaven, but only he who does the will of my father in heaven." -Matthew 7:21 "Make every effort to enter through the narrow door, because many, I tell you, will try to enter and will not be able to." -Luke 13:24 "Enter through the narrow gate, for wide is the gate broad is the road to destruction and many enter through it. But small is the gate and narrow is the path that leads to life, and only a few who find it." - Matthew 7:13-14 "I tell you that unless your righteousness surpasses that of the Pharisees and teachers of the law, you will certainly not enter the kingdom of heaven." -Matthew 5:20 "I tell you the truth, it is hard for a rich man to enter the kingdom of heaven. Again I tell you, it is easier for a camel to go through the eye of a needle than for a rich man to enter the kingdom of God." -Matthew 19:23-24

"I tell you the truth, no one can see the kingdom of God unless he is born again. Unless he is born of water and the spirit. Flesh gives birth to flesh, but the spirit gives birth to spirit. -John 3:3, 5-6 "I tell you the truth, anyone who will not receive the kingdom of God like a little child will never enter it." -Luke 18:17 "Unless you change and become like little children, you will never enter the kingdom of heaven. Therefore, whoever humbles himself like a child is the greatest in the kingdom of heaven." -Matthew 18:3-4

Do not become weary in doing good. For at the proper time you will reap a harvest if you do not give up. -Galatians 6:9 "When you give a luncheon or dinner, do not invite your friends, your brothers or relatives, or your rich neighbors; if you do, they may invite you back and so you will be repaid. But when you give a banquet, invite the poor, the crippled, the lame, the blind, and you will be blessed. Although they cannot repay you, you will be repaid at the resurrection of the righteous." -Luke 14:12-14

To those who by persistence in doing good seek glory, honor and immortality he will give eternal life! - Romans 2:7

"Do not store up for yourselves treasures on earth, where moth and rust destroy, where thieves break in and steal. But store up for yourselves treasure in heaven, where moth and rust do not destroy and thieves do not break in and steal. For where your treasure is, there your heart will be also!" -Matthew 6:19-21 "Do not work for food that spoils, but for food that endures to eternal life, which the son of man will give you. On him God the father has placed his seal of approval." -John 6:27

"I will give you the keys to the kingdom of heaven; whatever you bind on earth will be bound in heaven, and whatever you loose on earth will be loosed in heaven." - Matthew 16:19 "I tell you that men will have to give an account on the day of judgment for every careless word they have spoken. For by your words you will be acquitted, and by your words you will be condemned." -Matthew 12:36-37 Therefore judge nothing before the appointed time; wait until the Lord comes. He will bring to the light what is hidden in darkness and will expose the motives of men's hearts. At that time each will receive his praise from God. -1 Corinthians 4:5 For nothing in all creation is hidden from God's sight. Everything is uncovered and laid bare before the eyes of him who we must give account. -Hebrews 4:13

For it is time for judgment to begin with the family of God: and it begins with us. What will the outcome be for those who do not obey the gospel of God? And it will be hard for the righteous to be saved, what will become of the ungodly and the sinner. -1 Peter 4:17-18 For we must all appear before the judgment seat of Christ that each may receive what is due him for the things done while in the body. Whether good or bad. -2 Corinthians 5:10 For God will bring every deed into judgment, including every hidden thing, whether it is good or evil. -Ecclesiastes 12:14   Anyone who does wrong will be repaid for his wrong and there is no favoritism. -Colossians 3:25   For God does not show favoritism. -Romans 2:11

"The servant who knows his masters will and does not get ready or does not do what his master wants will be beaten with many blows. But the one who does not know and does things deserving punishment will be beaten with few blows. From everyone who has been given much, much will be demanded; and from the one who has been entrusted with much, much more will be asked." -Luke 12:47-48   If we deliberately keep on sinning after we have received the knowledge of the truth, no sacrifice for sin is left, but only a fearful expectation of judgment and of raging fire that will come and consume the enemies of God. -Hebrews 10:26-27

Anyone, then, who knows the good he ought to do and doesn't do it sins. -James 4:17   No one can lay any other foundation, other than the one already laid, which is Christ Jesus. If any man builds on this foundation using gold, silver, costly stones, wood, hay, or straw, his work will be shown for what it is, because the day will bring it to light. It will be revealed with fire, and the fire will test the quality of each man's work. If what he has built survives, he will receive his reward. If it is burned up he will suffer loss: he himself will be saved, but only as one escaping through the flames. - 1 Corinthians 3:11-15

"When the Son of Man comes in his glory, and all the angels with him, he will sit on his glorious throne. All the nations will be gathered before him, and he will separate the people one from another as a shepherd separates the sheep from the goats. He will put the sheep on his right and the goats on his left. "Then the King will say to those on his right, 'Come, you who are blessed by my Father; take your inheritance, the kingdom prepared for you since the creation of the world. For I was hungry and you gave me something to eat, I was thirsty and you gave me something to drink, I was a stranger and you invited me in, I needed clothes and you clothed me, I was sick and you looked after me, I was in prison and you came to visit me.' "Then the righteous will answer him, 'Lord, when did we see you hungry and feed you, or thirsty and give you something to drink? When did we see you a stranger and invite you in, or needing clothes and clothe you? When did we see you sick or in prison and go to visit you?' "The King will reply, 'Truly I tell you, whatever you did for one of the least of these brothers and sisters of mine, you did for me.' "Then he will say to those on his left, 'Depart from me, you who are cursed, into the eternal fire prepared for the devil and his angels. For I was hungry and you gave me nothing to eat, I was thirsty and you gave me nothing to drink, I was a stranger and you did not invite me in, I needed clothes and you did not clothe me, I was sick and in prison and you did not look after me.' "They also will answer, 'Lord, when did we see you hungry or thirsty or a stranger or needing clothes or sick or in prison, and did not help you?' "He will reply, 'Truly I tell you, whatever you did not do for one of the least of these, you did not do for me.' "Then they will go away to eternal punishment, but the righteous to eternal life." -Matthew 25:31-46

"Make every effort to enter through the narrow door, because many, I tell you, will try to enter and will not be able to." -Luke 13:24 "The kingdom of heaven is like treasure hidden in a field. When a man found it, he hid it again, and then in his joy sold all that he had and bought that field. Again the kingdom of heaven is like a merchant looking for fine pearls. When he found one of great value, he went away and sold everything he had and bought it." -Matthew 13:44-46 "Suppose one of you has a hundred sheep and loses one of them. Does he not leave the ninety-nine in the open country and go after the lost sheep until he finds it? And when he finds it, he joyfully puts it on his shoulders and goes home. Then he calls his friends and neighbors together and says, 'Rejoice with me; I have found my lost sheep.' I tell you that in the same way there will be more rejoicing in heaven over one sinner who repents than over ninety-nine righteous persons who do not need to repent." -Luke 15:4-7

"Or suppose a woman has ten silver coins and loses one. Does she not light a lamp, sweep the house and search carefully until she finds it? And when she finds it, she calls her friends and neighbors together and says, 'Rejoice with me; I have found my lost coin.' In the same way, I tell you, there is rejoicing in the presence of the angels of God over one sinner who repents." -Luke 15:8-10

But mark this: there will be terrible times in the last days. People will become lovers of themselves, lovers of money, boastful, proud, abusive, disobedient to their parents, ungrateful, unholy, without love, unforgiving, slanderous, without self-control, brutal, not lovers of good, treacherous, rash, conceited, lovers of pleasure rather than lovers of God. Having a form of godliness in them but denying its power. Have nothing to do with them. -2 Timothy 3:1-5

For the time will come when men will not put up with sound doctrine. Instead, to suit their own desires, they will gather around them a great number of teachers to say what their itching ears want to hear. They will turn their ears away from the truth and turn aside to myths. But you keep your head in all situations. Endure hardships, do the work of an evangelist. Discharge your duties of your ministry. -2 Timothy 4:3-5

"And the gospel of the kingdom will be preached in the whole world as a testimony to all nations and then the end will come." -Matthew 24:14

Then I saw a great white throne and him who was seated on it. The earth and the heavens fled from his presence, and there was no place for them. And I saw the dead, great and small, standing before the throne, and books were opened. Another book was opened, which is the book of life. The dead were judged according to what they had done as recorded in the books. The sea gave up the dead that were in it, and death and Hades gave up the dead that were in them, and each person was judged according to what they had done. Then death and Hades were thrown into the lake of fire. The lake of fire is the second death. Anyone whose name was not found written in the book of life was thrown into the lake of fire. He said to me: "It is done. I am the Alpha and the Omega, the Beginning and the End. To the thirsty I will give water without cost from the spring of the water of life. Those who are victorious will inherit all this, and I will be their God and they will be my children. But the cowardly, the unbelieving, the vile, the murderers, the sexually immoral, those who practice magic arts, the idolaters and all liars they will be consigned to the fiery lake of burning sulfur. This is the second death." -Revelation 20:11-15, 21:6-8

"The kingdom of heaven is like a man who sowed good seed in his field. But while everyone was sleeping, his enemy came and sowed weeds among the wheat, and went away. When the wheat sprouted and formed heads, then the weeds also appeared. "The owner's servants came to him and said, 'Sir, didn't you sow good seed in your field? Where then did the weeds come from?' "An enemy did this,' he replied. "The servants asked him, 'Do you want us to go and pull them up?' "No,' he answered, 'because while you are pulling the weeds, you may uproot the wheat with them. Let both grow together until the harvest. At that time I will tell the harvesters: First collect the weeds and tie them in bundles to be burned; then gather the wheat and bring it into my barn." -Matthew 13:24-30

"The one who sowed the good seed is the Son of Man. The field is the world, and the good seed stands for the people of the kingdom. The weeds are the people of the evil one, and the enemy who sows them is the devil. The harvest is the end of the age, and the harvesters are angels. As the weeds are pulled up and burned in the fire, so it will be at the end of the age. The Son of Man will send out his angels, and they will weed out of his kingdom everything that causes sin and all who do evil. They will throw them into the blazing furnace, where there will be weeping and gnashing of teeth. Then the righteous will shine like the sun in the kingdom of their Father. Whoever has ears, let them hear." -Matthew 13:37-43 "Once again, the kingdom of heaven is like a net that was let down into the lake and caught all kinds of fish. When it was full, the fishermen pulled it up on the shore. Then they sat down and collected the good fish in baskets, but threw the bad away. This is how it will be at the end of the age. The angels will come and separate the wicked from the righteous and throw them into the blazing furnace, where there will be weeping and gnashing of teeth." -Matthew 13:47-50

"Do not let your hearts be troubled. You believe in God; believe also in me. My Father's house has many rooms; if that were not so, would I have told you that I am going there to prepare a place for you? And if I go and prepare a place for you, I will come back and take you to be with me that you also may be where I am. You know the way to the place where I am going." -John 14:1-4

Questions for Reflection and Discussion

1. What are some ways that we can ensure that the ones we love and care about will make it to Heaven?

2. What was your happiest moment in your life that you have experienced so far? What were the types of emotions that you felt at that moment?

3. Were there people that you wished could have been there with you in that moment of happiness?

4. List the names of some people that you know that you want to make it into Heaven, but you aren't sure if they are saved.

5. How do you plan on helping others make sure that they will be able to enter Heaven with you?

CHAPTER TWELVE

UNITY IN WITNESSING

In this last chapter of this book we leave you with the last two final components that make the heart of God complete. As we went through this book we have talked about all different kinds of subjects that pertain to the heart of our Creator. We have studied and learned about all the different aspects of what God's heart really is and how we can grow and learn from these perspectives as a Christian in our daily walk. In this last chapter of the book we now bring you to closure on the heart of God by addressing these last two subjects. The first subject is witnessing. Witnessing is the by-product of a true relationship with the Lord. When we seek out our Heavenly Creator and develop a real intimate relationship with Him, we establish a trust and reliance in Him. Having that kind of sense of security in the Lord, naturally draws us to want to share with others about how having a relationship with God has not only helped us, but ultimately has changed our lives.

The Lord has the desire to help all of those who are willing to seek Him out. That is why it is our responsibility as Christians to bring the light of Christ to those who don't know about Him. Just as much as God has been pleased to help us out and interact with us, He also desires to have those same interactions with the whole entire rest of the world. Whether we like it or not people are going to die and go to hell. God doesn't want anyone to go to hell and that is where we come into the picture by introducing the Gospel to everyone we know so that they can have the same life changing opportunity that we have. So that they too can experience salvation and be able to enter the kingdom of heaven as well.

Wisdom from God's Heart

We are therefore Christ's ambassadors, as though God were making his appeal through us. We implore you on Christ's behalf: Be reconciled to God. -2 Corinthians 5:20 I pray that your partnership with us in the faith may be effective in deepening your understanding of every good thing we share for the sake of Christ. -Philemon 1:6 Through Jesus, therefore, let us continually offer to God a sacrifice of praise—the fruit of lips that openly profess his name. And do not forget to do good and to share with others, for with such sacrifices God is pleased. -Hebrews 13:15-16 Let us not become weary in doing good, for at the proper time we will reap a harvest if we do not give up. -Galatians 6:9 The LORD detests those whose hearts are perverse, but he delights in those whose ways are blameless. -Proverbs 11:20

God is able to bless you abundantly, so that in all things at all times, having all that you need, you will abound in every good work. - 2 Corinthians 9:8 The fruit of the righteous is a tree of life, and the one who is wise saves lives. - Proverbs 11:30 So neither the one who plants nor the one who waters is anything, but only God, who makes things grow. The one who plants and the one who waters have one purpose, and they will each be rewarded according to their own labor. -1 Corinthians 3:7-8 Remember this: Whoever sows sparingly will also reap sparingly, and whoever sows generously will also reap generously. Each of you should give what you have decided in your heart to give, not reluctantly or under compulsion, for God loves a cheerful giver. And God is able to bless you abundantly, so that in all things at all times, having all that you need, you will abound in every good work. As it is written: "They have freely scattered their gifts to the poor; their righteousness endures forever." Now he who supplies seed to the sower and bread for food will also supply and increase your store of seed and will enlarge the harvest of your righteousness. You will be enriched in every way so that you can be generous on every occasion, and through us your generosity will result in thanksgiving to God. -2 Corinthians 9:6-11

In your hearts revere Christ as Lord. Always be prepared to give an answer to everyone who asks you to give the reason for the hope that you have. But do this with gentleness and respect, keeping a clear conscience, so that those who speak maliciously against your good behavior in Christ may be ashamed of their slander. -1 Peter 3:15-16 If you remain in me and my words remain in you, ask whatever you wish, and it will be done for you. This is to my Father's glory, that you bear much fruit, showing yourselves to be my disciples. -John 15:7-8 If you spend yourselves in behalf of the hungry and satisfy the needs of the oppressed, then your light will rise in the darkness, and your night will become like the noonday. The LORD will guide you always; he will satisfy your needs in a sun-scorched land and will strengthen your frame. You will be like a well-watered garden, like a spring whose waters never fail. -Isaiah 58:10-11 Whoever turns a sinner from the error of their way will save them from death and cover over a multitude of sins. - James 5:20

10 HELPFUL TIPS FOR WITNESSING

1. Set a good example! (Read 1 Peter 2:11)

2. Study the Bible and seek God with all your HEART! (Read Psalm 1:1-2, Psalm 34:10, Proverbs 4:5, 2:6, 4:6,11,13)

3. Memorize God's Word! When you have scripture memorized, God will speak to you with those scriptures. You can't be an effective witness without having scriptures ingrained in your hearts and minds. (Read Matt. 5:14)

4. Spend time in prayer. Pray for guidance, patience and compassion towards those you witness and minister to. (Read James 5:16, Proverbs 15:29, 8)

5. Spend time Praising God. Praise acknowledges God, brings you into God's presence, moves God, strengthens your spirit, defeats the attack of the enemy, pleases God. (Read Psalm 18:3, 25, 29)

6. Know who your struggle is against! (Read Ephesians 6:12, 1 Peter 5:8)

7. Always be prepared! Be alert and self-controlled, keep a tight reign on your tongue, don't be easily angered, and don't be easily provoked, the devil will use anger from the person you are witnessing to provoke you to anger so you give up on that person.

8. Always have your tools handy! (make sure you carry a bible at all times, take an extra you never know when you will be able to give it away, Make sure you are sharing kind words of love and compassion)

9. Use these scriptures in this order to help with your witnessing John 14:21,23   Jeremiah 29:13, Romans 3:23-25, Hebrews 5:9, Acts 2:38, 1John3:8

10. Remember not to be afraid or nervous, God is with you! God will guide in you in these situations. When a person is seeking after the truth God will open up their heart to receive the knowledge you are just the tool that he will use to make it happen.

UNITY

The last part of this chapter is on unity and it is really quite simple. In order for us to be effective as Christians in spreading the Gospel we need to be unified. If we as Christians can't be together in one heart and in one mind then our belief system won't be attractive to any outsider no matter if it is the truth or not. The only goal the devil has when it comes to Christians is to divide and conquer. We all need to have one purpose, which is also God's purpose. God wants us all to have a strong relationship with Him. It's that simple. If we focused all of our energy on having a strong relationship with Him the whole world could be reached with the Gospel of our Lord Jesus Christ.

Wisdom from God's Heart

He made known to us the mystery of his will according to his good pleasure, which he purposed in Christ, to be put into effect when the times reach their fulfillment—to bring unity to all things in heaven and on earth under Christ. -Ephesians 1:9-10 I appeal to you, brothers and sisters, in the name of our Lord Jesus Christ, that all of you agree with one another in what you say and that there be no divisions among you, but that you be perfectly united in mind and thought. -1 Corinthians 1:10 If a kingdom is divided against itself, that kingdom cannot stand. If a house is divided against itself, that house cannot stand. -Mark 3:24-25 Make every effort to keep the unity of the Spirit through the bond of peace. There is one body and one Spirit, just as you were called to one hope when you were called; one Lord, one faith, one baptism; one God and Father of all, who is over all and through all and in all. -Ephesians 4:3-6

So Christ himself gave the apostles, the prophets, the evangelists, the pastors and teachers, to equip his people for works of service, so that the body of Christ may be built up until we all reach unity in the faith and in the knowledge of the Son of God and become mature, attaining to the whole measure of the fullness of Christ. Then we will no longer be infants, tossed back and forth by the waves, and blown here and there by every wind of teaching and by the cunning and craftiness of people in their deceitful scheming. Instead, speaking the truth in love, we will grow to become in every respect the mature body of him who is the head, that is, Christ. -Ephesians 4:11-15 My goal is that they may be encouraged in heart and united in love, so that they may have the full riches of complete understanding, in order that they may know the mystery of God, namely, Christ, in whom are hidden all the treasures of wisdom and knowledge. -Colossians 2:2-3 May the God who gives endurance and encouragement give you the same attitude of mind toward each other that Christ Jesus had, so that with one mind and one voice you may glorify the God and Father of our Lord Jesus Christ. Accept one another, then, just as Christ accepted you, in order to bring praise to God. -Romans 15:5-7

Therefore if you have any encouragement from being united with Christ, if any comfort from his love, if any common sharing in the Spirit, if any tenderness and compassion, then make my joy complete by being like-minded, having the same love, being one in spirit and of one mind. -Philippians 2:1-2 So then, just as you received Christ Jesus as Lord, continue to live your lives in him, rooted and built up in him, strengthened in the faith as you were taught, and overflowing with thankfulness. See to it that no one takes you captive through hollow and deceptive philosophy, which depends on human tradition and the elemental spiritual forces of this world rather than on Christ. For in Christ all the fullness of the Deity lives in bodily form, and in Christ you have been brought to fullness. He is the head over every power and authority. -Colossians 2:6-10

QUESTIONS FOR REFLECTION AND DISCUSSION

1. What are some of the ways that Christians can become divided amongst each other?

2. What are some ways that we could help all the local churches in the area becomes more united together.

3. What are some tips that will be very helpful for you to use when you witness to a non-believer?

4. Make a list of people that you know that you would like to share the gospel with and set a goal of a date and time in which you intend to fulfill that goal.

CONCLUSION

I hope that in reading this book, it has totally changed your mindset and perspective on your thoughts and how you view what your purpose and calling in life should be. I hope that this has given you a better understanding of who God is and what the "BIG PICTURE" is all about. If you would like to share your experiences of reading this book or if you have any questions or comments please feel free to email me at <u>wkoops78@hotmail.com</u>

NOTES

NOTES

Notes